The Storm

The Storm

Navigating the New Economy

Léon Courville

Translated by Donald Winkler
Foreword by John Ralston Saul

Published in 1995 by
Stoddart Publishing Co. Limited
34 Lesmill Road
Toronto, Canada
M3B 2T6
Tel. (416) 445-3333
Fax (416) 445- 5967

Stoddart Books are available for bulk purchase for sales promotions, premiums, fundraising, and seminars. For details, contact the **Special Sales Department** at the above address.

Canadian Cataloguing in Publication Data

Courville, Léon
The storm: navigating the new economy

Translation of: Piloter dans la tempête.
Includes index.
ISBN 0-7737-2881-3

1. Industrial management . 2. Managerial economics.
3. Organizational change. 4. Economic history –
1990– I. Title.

HD33.C6813 1995   658   C95-930671-4

Cover Design: Bill Douglas/The Bang
Computer Graphics: Tannice Goddard/S.O. Networking
Printed and bound in Canada

*Stoddart Publishing gratefully acknowledges the support of the
Canada Council, the Ontario Ministry of Culture, Tourism,
and Recreation, Ontario Arts Council, and Ontario Publishing Centre
in the development of writing and publishing in Canada.*

CONTENTS

FOREWORD

A LETTER TO THE AUTHOR

M. Léon Courville
Montréal, Québec

Dear Léon Courville:

I have just finished *The Storm*, which I must say I enjoyed. It seems to me that you are quite right on the questions of growth and globalization, the importance of incertitude, and problems associated with "managers."

Your assertion that "the opening up of markets remained compatible with political and economic stability as long as markets continued to grow" summarizes many of our problems, even if few contemporary economists are able to face up to this conundrum. And as for "businesses now call themselves organizations" — marvellous.

There are times when I feel a bit less optimistic than you. The neoconservatives, with their ideological vision of the market, have constructed a biblical version of capitalism from strands of simplistic ideas which have, precisely, rendered globalization inevitable.

I agree that the creativity of employees — of "mobilized workers" — is essential. But we are increasingly moving in the opposite direction — towards instability of employment. I can't see why an employee would invest his creativity in a business in which he is not a participant and from which he can be easily fired. This is one of the most important contradictions in our economic evolution.

You are right to say that one solution would be for executives to create their own businesses. But two large obstacles remain — obstacles that you know better than I: management schools are more likely to produce employees than entrepreneurs, and money is more available to large organizations than to smaller and newer businesses.

In fact, all of this hinges on how one deals with changes in technology. You broached the question very well towards the end of your book. These changes are undoubtedly inevitable. To refuse them would be to be "Luddite." But the last time we opened this debate — during the eighteenth and nineteenth centuries — the result was simultaneously great wealth and both social and political instability. This instability produced communism, social confrontations, disorder, and violence everywhere, to say nothing of an unprecedented ferocity. Throughout the West we barely escaped revolution. And now, today, having scarcely emerged from these divisions, we are plunging headlong right back into them again. I am convinced that the obligation of contemporary elites is to find a way through these massive changes without slipping back into a society of confrontation and battle.

As you can see, your book interested me greatly. I'm delighted it is now being published in English. Bay Street certainly needs to read it!

With best wishes,

John Ralston Saul
Toronto, Ontario

PREFACE

This book, intended for interested observers (not necessarily specialists) in the realm of business and economics, is like a fresco: sketched in bold strokes, it contrasts old management methods with emerging ones. But first and foremost, it explains the old economic order in order to make the new order stand out boldly.

My former university colleagues will have to pardon the shortcuts I have taken where history, theory, and schools of thought are concerned. I have chosen to indicate how the different elements connect, rather than to describe them individually in detail. I wanted to go to the heart of the matter without overwhelming the reader with subtleties and specifics that would have added little to my argument. I want specialists to see the whole picture. But it is non-specialists in particular I had in mind, for whom I tried to make this book accessible and easy to digest.

I would like to thank, above all, Jean-Paul Léjeune, who

recorded my words and gave them their initial form. His patience, tenacity, and especially his ability to listen, direct research, suggest examples, and organize the text, were an enormous help.

I benefitted from the comments and observations of many people, including Michel Bélanger, Reuven Brenner, Jean-Paul Caron, Marcel Côté, Gérard Coulombe, Wendy Dobson, Jean-Claude Gagnon, Luce Gosselin, Pierre Lemieux, John Saul, Dominique Vachon, and, from l'École des HÉC, Jacques Fortin, François Leroux, Michel Patry, as well as Alain Chanlat, who contributed to the development — startling, at times — of some of the ideas to be found in this book. To all, my deep appreciation.

Finally, my thanks to André Bérard, the most eloquent and persuasive of teachers. Without his help in putting these ideas to the test, this book would not exist.

Léon Courville
Montréal, Québec

The Storm

Analysis destroys wholes. Some things,
magic things, are meant to stay whole.
If you look at their pieces, they go away.

Robert James Waller
The Bridges of Madison County

Nor is time granted oftener to empires than to men
to learn from past errors.
Although a weaver would wish to mend his web
or a clever calculator would correct his mistakes,
and the artist would try to retouch his masterpiece
if still imperfect or slightly damaged,
Nature prefers to start again from the very clay,
from chaos itself,
and this horrible waste is what we term the natural order.

Marguerite Yourcenar
Hadrian's Memoirs

INTRODUCTION

The postwar years were a remarkable era. Blessed with unprecedented progress, the idea of unlimited development became part of our worldview. In our march towards affluence, each day was to be better than the last. But now easy economic growth has disappeared; the economy no longer can fulfil the aspirations so deeply ingrained in Western society over the last 100 years. We have not yet come to terms with the impact this change will have, nor with the adjustment that will be required if we are to respond constructively to the new economic reality.

Total quality, just-in-time, quality circles, profit-sharing, accountability, outsourcing, industrial strategy, privatization: entrepreneurs and managers in both the private and public sectors have grown accustomed over the last two decades to a passing parade of business trends. The purpose of these numerous watchwords was to help us avoid the hazards set in our path by a new peril, the globalization of markets.

But in the long run, none of that has spared us the restructuring that continues to afflict virtually all the Western economies following the recent recession. Unlike other troughs in the economic cycle, this difficult period is particularly tenacious, and is accompanied by economic, political, and social disorder everywhere on the planet. The economy's reins have slipped from our hands.

New codes of conduct are being defined here and there in business and in political programs, marking a radical departure from traditional managerial methods. A flawed reading of the environment makes for bad decisions, that we know. Which explains the current vogue for learning to read all over again.

For the last 100 years or so, our understanding of the universe was grounded in sustained economic growth, and growing political and social stability, worldwide. From that we derived our vision of unending progress. Business, unions, governments: all set out to conquer an Everest that was easy of access and gratifying to climb.

The symbiosis between our actions and the environment has been broken. For proof one need only note the gloom of managers and business leaders who have no more confidence in their prognostications than in the spin of a roulette wheel. Note also the crisis in confidence on the part of voters, who no longer understand their politicians, who no longer believe in them. A recent poll sponsored by the Québec Employers' Council indicates that only 9% of Québecers trust their political leaders, by far the lowest results ever registered.

Today we are imprisoned in a giant closed system, a single market with no growth; the challenge no longer is to strive higher but to relieve one's neighbour of part of his place in the sun — while making sure that no one is able to return the favour. We can no longer hope to find new markets, we can only infringe on those of others (which implies that others will also try to lay hands on ours). This heightened competition worldwide is what forces us to be creative, to respond instantly, whatever may occur. Of course, there are places where the sun still shines, but they are increasingly rare. We must therefore conserve our energies, keep a close eye on our clients and competitors, and be prepared to react immediately, at the slightest provocation. This agility, this potential for rapid response, for adapting, requires a new type of organization: supple, light, committed to action.

In the past our challenge as managers was to ensure continuity, to mobilize our troops, to direct all our efforts towards the same goal, so that our business might progress more speedily than others as we sought new markets. Each company was on the way to its own "far west." This orderly universe has ceased to exist. Tom Peters, author of *In Search of Excellence*, is of the opinion that the context in which we must now manage our businesses is akin to chaos. To deal with chaos, we must from now on be able to act immediately, our reflexes honed by new circumstances, our reactions rapid, appropriate, spontaneous, unreflective.

Strategy is born from action, says Henry Mintzberg, another management analyst. Power must be returned to those who act. We must eliminate those positions that are only advisory and reflective, for by definition they risk being divorced from reality. Those who are close to the client, the supplier, and the market must provide solutions; because they are at the heart of the action, their reading of the situation is more acute.

In the past the primary function of managers was to think and plan, and their apostles transmitted their message to those who were delegated to act. Today, however, thought, reflection, knowledge, and action are all integrated; they are closely connected, practised by the same person. Middle management is shrinking. We are witnessing the end of hierarchies and, perhaps, of consultants.

Alain Minc talks of a new Middle Ages, echoing the American Robert S. Kaplan, who sees the first century of the coming millennium subsiding into destructive anarchy. Perhaps they are right. Perhaps, too, deep down, they are nostalgic for an extinct order they associate with progress, as if only this order could enable humanity to flourish.

In the meantime, we must not be defeatist. We must try something else. We must, above all, move ahead. The old order was established through an understanding of the old economy; in like manner, new guideposts and new modes of behaviour will be suggested by an understanding of the new economy. Some may talk of the Middle Ages, yes, but others may prefer the Renaissance.

Let us begin with a description of our old environment, and an account of how we learned to adapt to it. We will then outline the new economy and propose ways in which we must change if we want to survive and progress.

1

A RETURN TO ANARCHY

Market growth, political stability, a more affluent population, all favoured the emergence of hierarchical and planning-oriented businesses. But worldwide competition, political uncertainty, and a halt in growth have forced these same organizations to work for a symbiosis between themselves and the new environmental chaos for which they were never designed.

H ow sweet it was to run a company in 1970! The managers scurried to conferences such as the one organized by l'Institut de con-trôle de la gestion in Paris on how to control growth. At that time, not so long ago, economists looked forward to a leisure society in which we would consume ever greater amounts. And all before the year 2000, with a work week of only 20 hours! The world, at last politically and socially secure, would be showered with goods and services by global corporations, organized, automated, able to anticipate all our needs. Companies that applied their management techniques and undertook planning programs would be infallible — would deliver the best of all possible worlds, with no surprises, crises, or uncertainty. But today the dream has vanished: we live in a time of retrenchment. The leisure society never saw the light of day. As for the consumer society, emblematic of Western materialism's triumph, it is dead, talked about no more. It was, however, considered the purest product of the capitalist system. The markets fed off the consumer society and the consumer society nourished the markets by injecting them with ever more money. In a context of endless economic growth, life's very goal was to consume, and the aim of business was to produce ever more.

A SOCIETY OF SHEEP

Twenty, forty years ago, the little world of industrialists and merchants hadn't a worry in the world. Everything seemed so easy to sell. Money was there for the asking, an offshoot of growth or the magic of borrowing: governments set about mortgaging the future, freeing individuals from the need to think for themselves. Collective wealth seemed to promise infinite growth. Certain that the buyer would buy, we didn't have to bother being creative. For a long time consumers had to content themselves with a single kind of cola, a single type of shoes, Fords that came only in black, and so on.

Sales techniques were based on the models available. We showed clients what they ought to buy, and they bought, for in a society where there is money, not spending is suspect. Everyone has to show that he is spending in conformity with his social group. Consumers were flush with cash. Their tastes were predictable and conformist. It was easy to figure out what had to be produced, in what quantity, and at what price. Managers lived in perfect symbiosis with their economic, political, and social environment.

In the 1970s, however, the consumption-growth, growth-consumption spiral was broken, at least as it had been understood. John Kenneth Galbraith's age of opulence (*The Affluent Society*) began to break down, unexpectedly. Cracks appeared, and the production of goods did not give the results anticipated. With the economy no longer performing to expectations, governments began to print money to stimulate growth, forgetting that such actions are futile. Structural deficits in government became a reality. Certainly economic well-being was enhanced, but much of it was an illusion, and we were living on borrowed time. The French geneticist Albert Jacquard got it right when he described us, with respect to the future, as the greatest generation of thieves in all of history.

THE BEGINNING OF THE END

About this time, the Japanese began to penetrate our markets, targeting people who had less money, and who as a result were less affected by what was in fashion. Think of the toys, television sets, motorcycles, and cars they produced at the time. These people were marginal clients, of little interest to a system based on growth. It is no surprise that Japanese products were held in contempt by Western manufacturers.

There are, of course, many technical and financial factors that explain the Japanese success in the United States, in particular, their approach to marketing and the question of timing: they offered cheap, long-lasting products just as economic growth began to falter. In the 1980s the Japanese won over a more difficult, demanding — and unanticipated — clientele who had nothing in common, any longer, with the conformists of the consumer society. Now that wealth has stopped accumulating, clients have become exacting, difficult, capricious. That is why managers are now so preoccupied with them. That is also why no one any longer speaks of the consumer society.

AT THE MERCY OF THE MARKET

Markets have opened up and technology has made anything possible. As a result, the consumer has never known such a vast variety of products. He has become the true arbiter wherever there is competition; it is he who determines who wins and who loses. He limits his purchases, avoids taking risks, and seeks out the product that meets his needs or desires most exactly.

With the tables turned, some established corporations are in total disarray. Their marketing methods and management techniques are no longer appropriate. Manufacturers, accustomed to mass production, have to show more creativity and flexibility in order to respond to a dual challenge: to satisfy specific needs and to produce cheaply. And as all the competitors are fighting over a market that has almost stopped expanding, they can only exchange clients — or steal them from each other.

The North American automobile industry has been turned upside down, and it is not alone. Television sets, video cassette recorders — American inventions, after all — are produced in Japan or elsewhere in Asia. It is the beginning of globalization; the opening up of markets renders obsolete old corporate structures, and makes the consumer once again supreme.

Again, Galbraith got it wrong. For him, the ease with which the industrial class was able to accumulate wealth, grow, sell more, encouraged the belief that production had prevailed over consumption. In the new industrial state, the American industrial class would be susceptible to a socialist, planned economy. Those who planned production planned the economy. Producers were relatively few; they were able to work out agreements, tacit or not, that would concentrate power or wealth in their hands. If Galbraith was right, it was not for long. The industrial class quickly fragmented. If competition, which tilts the balance in favour of clients, of consumers, did not come from within, it would come from without, and with a vengeance.

FOR EVERY WINNER, A LOSER

The age of opulence is dead! Look around: those who dreamed of a leisure society have never worked so hard to hang on to jobs that have never been so shaky. The future is no longer certain for anyone: corporations of worldwide reputation, such as IBM, GM, Renault, could very well disappear, or be radically transformed before the end of the decade.

In order to survive, these companies are espousing policies diametrically opposed to those they endorsed only five years earlier: they now talk of restructuring, layoffs, cutbacks. Governments speak the same language, and trim pensions, social assistance, and unemployment insurance just when the number of pensioners and unemployed is on the rise. Governments cast a greedy eye on health insurance, waiting only for the strategic moment to cut into it deeply.

And, as though planners didn't have enough problems, the opening up of markets has brought new players on the scene. We have embarked on a zero sum game; for every winner, there is now a loser.

To sell, it is no longer enough just to answer the consumers' needs. You have to give them more for their money. You have to set yourself apart from the competition, constantly developing new products to anticipate the buyers' desires, and in so doing, to outdistance your competitors.

The client, faced with this plethora of brand names, of replacement products, considers many more criteria in making his choice, criteria more complex than simple adherence to group behaviour. For purveyors of products and services, the puzzle is increasingly complex: how to foresee that in one month a competitor will come up with a model of air-pump running shoes that will win over customers who now swear only by the shoe with the streamlined sole I am currently offering.

A RETURN TO THE MIDDLE AGES

What threat are we facing? An economic depression, or the return to a new Middle Ages, akin to that era's frequent periods of conflict, uprisings, wars, and secessions between the fall of the Roman Empire and the Renaissance. The question may appear preposterous, since for three generations we have experienced growth and increasing cohesion in the international economy. Why should the process stop now? Because all civilizations have known periods of growth, unification, and stability, followed invariably by a return to disorder, by a turning in on oneself, by political, social, and economic uncertainty.

Mankind is blessed from time to time with periods when it is favoured by the gods, when new ideas and technological progress provide a certain coherence, a reassuring equilibrium. Harmony prevails, and growth is rapid. Ancient Greece gave us plane geometry, classic technical innovations such as the endless screw, new ways of reasoning, the fundamentals of democracy, and the foundations of exact science, such as the Archimedes Principle. The Romans established the first great avenues of communication in Europe. They developed a civil code whose principles live on in the Napoleonic Code. They disseminated the alphabet we still use today.

We have to go back as far as the Renaissance to trace the roots of modern physics, chemistry, and mathematics, as refined by Newton, Lavoisier, Descartes, and dozens of others. All these periods were characterized by great technical discoveries, and a shift in the understanding of the universe according to the principles these discoveries brought to the fore.

But all these civilizations ultimately declined into anarchy, once their luminaries realized that the social and economic context was eluding them, no longer matching their vision, divorcing them from reality.

So it was in Asiatic antiquity and in the great South American civilizations. These periods were shot through with troubled moments, when ideas circulated with difficulty. Peoples opposed each other in military and commercial wars, without any unifying idea prevailing over political and philosophical divisions.

When we observe the inability of the United Nations to maintain peace in Europe and Africa, the painful GATT talks, the United States' diminished sway over the Western world, the resurgence of isolationist economic blocs, we may well fear a return to a medieval period. After a century dedicated to reducing international political instability, a period when everything conspired to create a balance never before attained on the world stage, a century of increased stability, we seem to be relapsing into anarchy.

This medieval pitfall can of course be averted and prevented. But we must understand what is now at stake and not opt for isolation and protectionism over creativity, the only valid response to the shock of the 1980s and early '90s.

2

THE PLANNERS
IN DISARRAY

Without the discovery of oil, and then computer
technology, the Industrial Revolution would never
have produced the collective wealth of the 20th
century. Now we are seeking a new driving force
that will lead to postindustrial prosperity.

In 1992 and 1993, distinguished heads
rolled in the developed world. Some, such
as Rod Canion, founder and chief executive officer of
Compaq, had been cited as role models in master of
business administration courses. Others, such as Bernard
Tapie, had exemplified dynamic management and all-out
commercial development. John Ackers, president and chief
executive officer of IBM, he who had changed the course of
the corporation that it might recover its profitability, lost his
post. The presidents of Johnson Products, Paramount
Pictures, Time Warner, Digital, General Motors, all were victims of a mania that infected panicky boardrooms as
profits collapsed and collective wealth evaporated.

This impoverishment — which translates into severe debt
in most developed countries — has brought in its wake dis-
ruptions that cannot be controlled by standard management

techniques. The military supremacy of the United States is no longer enough to guarantee peace in Western countries. Governments' financial problems oblige them to dismantle some of their social programs. This entails not only the risk of unrest, but also a decline in the buying power of consumers. The globalization of markets only exacerbates the trend towards an endless procession of new products, new technology, and new services, all of which make planning impossible.

Is this only a temporary development, or does it indicate a profound and long-lasting change, with which we will have to live for many years to come?

LEARNING FROM THE GREEKS

To explain the birth of civilizations, the Greeks had a legend, that of Prometheus, the god who stole fire from the gods and offered it to man. He imparted the knowledge that would make it possible to found a society, to build and to see into the future. The Romanian economist Georgescu Roegen takes up this idea when he explains that the earth is entropic: it closes in on itself and contracts, has a tendency to degenerate. From time to time something happens that pushes back the frontiers, wards off the contraction, and creates a new dynamic as though a Prometheus had arrived bringing with him a life force that would stimulate growth once again. His blessed invention was fire; the 20th century would perhaps know another.

THE INDUSTRIAL REVOLUTION
BEFORE ENERGY

A little over a century ago we received a new gift from the gods. At that time, the Western world had begun its

Industrial Revolution, but most of the population still lived in misery, because we did not yet have the energy to operate our new industrial motor. In the middle of the nineteenth century, the West seemed backed into an economic corner, as the testimony of eight-year-old Sarah Gooder, makes clear. She worked in an English coal mine in 1842. Her testimony is recorded in Lord Ashley's *Report of Commissioners* dealing with the employment of children in mines, which was tabled in the English parliament. Sarah was responsible for opening the air doors at the Gawber shaft, and described how she had to work in the dark, from 3:30 or 4:00 in the morning until 5:30 in the afternoon. One of her "colleagues," Patience Kershaw, seventeen years old, explained that the bald spot on her head came from pushing mine-cars weighing 150 kilos a mile or more back and forth, underground, eleven hours a day. Zola's *Germinal* was inspired by the real world of the second half of the last century.

That was life for most people in the West a century and a half ago. Those spared this fate were the peasants, living independently from hand to mouth on their farms, and a small group of industrialists. The majority would end up in misery, working in factories, exploited by one of the affluent few. For most of mankind, only 100 years ago, one day's labour could barely put bread on the next day's table. The political universe was akin to a state of war. We had invented the Industrial Revolution, but we lacked that life force from the gods that would bring us prosperity.

A GIFT FROM THE GODS

Fortunately, Prometheus came back to earth Saturday evening, August 28, 1859, at Titusville in Pennsylvania. There, "Colonel" Drake had installed his first derrick. That night, the drill shaft forced its way into a deposit of naphtha that would soon generate 1,500 litres of oil per day. A few weeks later, the price per barrel sank from $20 to $10. A year and a half later, it was only 10 cents, and it finally stabilized for the next 100 years at between 70 cents and $1.60. In 1859, production reached 270 tons per year, rising to 400,000 in less than three years.

As soon as oil was discovered, a few industrialists, a bit more farsighted than the others, immediately grasped the significance of low-priced energy; they understood the new rules of the game, and they applied them. John D. Rockefeller, for example, came to dominate the refining of oil, then its shipment, storage, commerce, and finally its production. He invented, after a fashion, modern vertical and horizontal integration. It was a winning formula that served as a model for the next century. The economy was reconceived, enabling business leaders to live in harmony with their environment. A new era of progress was at hand, one that would bring wealth and stability.

The discovery of oil at the end of the nineteenth century was one of those stimuli that retarded entropy by greatly increasing the value of the resources we possessed. A new way of looking at management was born.

POWER TO THE IMAGINATION

Immediately, clever minds invented innumerable business opportunities. The extraordinary impetus that oil gave to industry was reflected in the field of technical research: up to 1860, the American Patent Office had granted 36,000 letters patent; from 1860 to 1890, it registered 400,000! Among these inventions, some would play a crucial role in economic development. The dynamo, conceived in 1869 by the Belgian Zénobe Gramme, was perfected by the American Thomas Edison. Energy could now instantly travel long distances; the invention of the telephone by Alexander Graham Bell in 1876 became feasible. Fifty years later, six million telephones were already in use in the United States.

Imagine yourself in the skin of a West Coast industrialist in the U.S. at that time. Instead of having to learn about new technical developments or new markets by sending messages via the Wells-Fargo stagecoach, or a rider for the Pony-Express, you could now question directly, by telephone, whoever had the information you needed, even if they were on the other side of the continent. Your market was no longer limited to your city and its environs but took in the entire territory. Soon, steamships would make the whole world accessible. And then, in the wake of the automobile . . .

The local entrepreneur who operated in a stable market found himself plunged into an expanding world: frontiers drew back, clients were ever more numerous and increasingly wealthy. Put anything at all on the market and there would always be someone to buy it. Economic uncertainty disappeared. With enough experience, it was possible to create more and more exact models to predict sales, organize production, ship products.

A unifying vision of the universe was now possible; now one could predict growth. All that was needed to navigate in a perfectly predictable sea was international political stability.

STABILITY AT ITS STRONGEST

Industrialists and merchants, knowing that political stability was crucial to their future, tirelessly exerted pressure on their governments to achieve it. Of course, there were wars, but after each one the world found itself more united, less fragmented than before.

The aftereffects of the Second World War were especially advantageous to Western business. A new, stronger stability gave rise to stronger organizations and systems of control. Agreements such as the North Atlantic Treaty Organization (NATO), the Common Market, the Warsaw Pact could only have been reached in the context of peace. Nationalism would have blocked the way. There was only one drawback: the victors could not agree on how to ensure stability. In the East, the Soviets relied on the authority of the state. They organized the economy, more or less as we structure our industrial conglomerates: the head office — the Supreme Soviet — planned, organized, and controlled the whole show.

In the West, we opted for a free market. But we took care to set up regulatory systems, for it was important that the world remain stable and that the future become predictable. We were faithful to the Beveridge Report, from the London School of Economics, which in the 1930s had begun to weave the social security net. After all, poverty had to be avoided in order to ensure stability.

The frenetic quest for economic stability resulted in theories that approached the absurd, such as that of automatic stabilizers. It was claimed, for example, that when unemployment climbs, insurance payments increase, which forces governments to spend more in a period of growth; unemployment insurance is thus an automatic stabilizer. The same held true for graduated income tax: it was an economic stabilizer. Stabilization was the doctrine of the moment, both in economics and in management.

Already in 1944, while the war still raged in Europe, the Bretton Woods agreements established a single standard for Western monies: the dollar. The concern to limit fluctuations was so great, the approach to our economic universe so widely shared, that it took only four days to finalize those agreements. With the exchange rates fixed, fiscal stability could become a reality. The United States would assume the role of both policeman and banker to the Western world.

With stability achieved, growth was assured: the West, its reconstruction in full swing, represented a tremendous outlet for the United States, while for other countries the smallest fragment of the American market constituted an extraordinary windfall compared with their own domestic market. For three decades, imports in the United States represented only 3 to 5% of the gross national product.

In the East, as in the West, the goal was the same: to ensure stability. Confrontation between the two blocs was decisive in that regard, freezing the sphere of influence of each for 40 years. There were conflicts here and there, but never in a region crucial to world economic development or commerce. Yalta did more than split the world in two; it created two great zones of stability.

GROWTH AT ANY COST

It was perfectly clear that growth, too, had to be assured. Two principles were invoked: open markets and an increase in buying power. The General Agreement on Tariffs and Trade negotiations, undertaken in 1948, would little by little do away with obstacles to the circulation of goods and services.

It was then agreed that a growth in buying power could do with a little encouragement. The 1950s in North America saw the invention of the credit card, while the Europeans established a banking system that was more and more unified and effective. The result on both sides of the Atlantic was to increase the indebtedness of populations, enterprises, and states. Growth need no longer wait for an increase in wealth; it anticipated it.

The postwar period also saw the rapid development of computer technology, the ideal tool for planning and control. Thanks to oil, it was possible to manufacture the synthetic products needed to make computers, and to produce the huge quantities of electrical energy they required.

Computer science was the second Promethean gift in less than a century. Now, managers could increase their capacity to control information, to look ahead, to plan. The cost of information per unit dropped a thousand times in a few years, and virtually everything was subject to constant control: production and sales data, the tastes of consumers, the most refined of economic indicators.

It is astonishing to see, in retrospect, that we used computer technology primarily to enhance our powers of control and planning. Production benefitted from automation only much later on, and is still trying to catch up. This is simply because when the universe is predictable, the best way to live in harmony with it is to plan for the future.

These management principles, in the 20 years following the war, were applied in an environment for which they had been conceived: political stability, market growth, means of control and planning that were extraordinarily effective. Those three factors encouraged a belief in the possibility of unlimited progress. The freeing up of markets would enable populations to trade more, and so increase their production and their well-being without having to work any harder. Doubtless they would work less. And so the dream arose first of a consumer society, then a leisure society, because this evolution corresponded perfectly to our understanding of the Western world.

PROMETHEUS DOESN'T KNOCK THREE TIMES

We ought to have seen the collapse of the 1970s coming. In fact, during the 1960s, growth in the non-communist world stood at 4.9%. The following decade, it was down to 3.8%, and it fell to 2.9% in the 1980s. The growth per person in gross national product went from 2.8% in the '60s to 1.1% in the '80s.

The signs were clear: growth was slowing down. We needed a new stimulus to get it going again. We needed a catalyst comparable to the discovery of oil. There were those who were quite aware of this. One need only note the enormous sums invested to find new sources of energy that would be less expensive and more abundant than oil. It was no secret that abundant energy was the key to the remarkable growth the world had experienced.

Those who would control the new less-expensive and more abundant energy would be tomorrow's winners. Many governments, as of the '50s, undertook ambitious projects in the area of nuclear fission, then solar power, biomass, tides, sea swells, and so on. But all in vain: the costs were no lower. We might even ask ourselves today if the costs of this research were not greater than the benefits that accrued.

At present, research is directed towards cold fusion. But the researchers must constantly extend their deadlines. The most optimistic among them do not expect to be producing electricity from nuclear fusion before 2020. Many think it will not happen before the middle of the 21st century, since the date is regularly put back by 20 years, and then another 20. And the investment sums needed are such that only the great international consortiums can afford them.

We must therefore content ourselves with, at best, the same energy supply as we have now. Prometheus does not seem ready, yet, to offer us another gift.

THE GLOBALIZATION NOBODY WANTED

Because we thought that growth would continue, we did not foresee that the expansion of markets would lead to their globalization. No one wanted *this* globalization, because it made a mockery of our systems of stabilization, it brought back disorder, it conflicted with our understanding of the world. The opening up of markets remained compatible with political and economic stability as long as the markets continued to grow. But when countries, in order to maintain their growth, were forced to trespass on the markets of their neighbours — and in particular on the U.S. market — nationalisms resurfaced.

Since the 1970s, our economic history has been marked by disputes over countervailing duties imposed, each in turn, by the United States and Europe on metal products, agricultural produce, wine, and so on. The same war is being waged between the United States and Japan, and between Japan and Europe. The markets have, behind our backs, undermined stability. The equation — growth + stability = wealth — no longer factors out.

Look at what is happening with GATT. During the first weeks of 1993, we saw hordes of French farmworkers and fishermen demolish distribution centres for imported products. These demonstrations were more like revolts, since they consisted in pillaging, if not putting to the torch, businesses that imported agricultural products. Tons of goods were destroyed, to the tune of many millions of dollars, ruining entrepreneurs who were simply doing business in accord with national and international regulations.

What was the reason for these outbreaks, perpetrated in full view of a passive French government? A divergence of views, that is all, between Europeans and Americans, on the role of agriculture! The Americans maintain that agricultural exploitation is an industry like any other, to be managed according to principles of planning and organization, with economies of scale and all the classic management techniques. Europe has succeeded in establishing a system that protects agricultural workers and creates a certain harmony within the economic bloc. What is more, Europeans see agricultural workers as gardeners in the countryside: they are responsible for irrigating the fields, taking care of the land, preserving the appearance of the European landscape, an important touristic — and therefore economic — birthright.Europeans think they must continue to pay agricultural workers for these activities.

These opposing views could exist side by side as long as markets were sufficiently discrete. But now one must choose between markets and stability. And it is the markets that have the upper hand.

A RETURN TO THE GREAT TRADING BLOCS

"Enough is enough: we've had cars from Japan, pyjamas from the Philippines, bicycles and sandals from China, television sets from Korea, computer chips from Malaysia, and so on. Now we're being swamped by goods from Eastern Europe." These words, taken from *L'Expansion* of May 1993, clearly indicate how fed up European business leaders are with the globalization of markets.

Europe is closing in on itself, opening its markets only to enterprises that respect its own rules. Will the United States allow European countries to dictate how it regulates its banking system? Let's not be naive! The U.S. will retaliate with embargoes and countervailing duties. Thirty years ago its economic supremacy would have afforded it the last word, but today things have changed.

Instability has set in even within the great economic blocs. For 20 years Europeans have been speaking of a Europe of regions. The ultimate objective is that states disappear, creating a European common market, with regions whose powers would essentially be cultural. But things have been evolving otherwise. We are beginning to see not only regions but cities competing for economic supremacy. Strasbourg and Brussels are in a struggle to the death for the title of European capital. Montpellier and Nice are investing exorbitant sums to create ultramodern industrial centres as they strive for economic supremacy in the south of France. Rotterdam and Anvers are in a bitter fight over maritime traffic in the North Sea, while London and Bonn both aspire to be the financial hub of the continent.

North America is not to be outdone. A striking example is North American free trade, which spells out draconian rules of origin in the automobile, textile, and other sectors. In order to benefit from free trade in Canada, the United States, and Mexico, cars must be composed of parts whose origin is 62.5% North American!

And let us not forget the numerous disputes that occur every year between Canada and its southern neighbour over softwood lumber, pork, milk products, and so on. As for the expansion of North American free trade, many U.S. congressmen contend that to allow the marketplace free rein would constitute a threat to the stability of the American economy.

THE WALTZ OF THE CEOS

That is why the North American economy took so long to recover after the 1991 recession. In fact, businesses, as they restructured themselves, continued to be plagued by stagnant sales and weak profits, which is the reason for the tens of thousands of layoffs, the forsaking of certain operations, and the closing of factories. Presidents of great corporations were replaced by the dozens. In 1992-93, twelve of fifteen heads of automobile companies across the world were replaced; top executives were let go by the thousands; unemployment, a creature of the recession, barely declined; important firms once cited as role models around the world for the quality of their management turned their backs on the principles that had brought them their success.

Europe, hit by the recession two years after North America, is far removed from the optimism that had countries looking to a great and prosperous common market starting in 1992! Today, talk of Europe among politicians is much more circumspect.

If we turn to the international scene we find a United Nations wracked by dissension, powerless to impose peace in Bosnia, Somalia, Nagorno-Karabakh, Iraq. We find hotbeds of tension in all the countries of the Near East and North Africa. An explosion of the South African powder keg is to be feared. So are new barriers rising up between the great economic blocs of North America, Japan, and Europe.

The economic boom that accompanied the discovery of oil only lasted a short time. Entropy has once more got the upper hand and our vision of an ever-expanding global economy no longer corresponds to reality. We do not know how to interpret what is happening. That is the source of our great disarray, and our inability to make effective decisions.

Is it any wonder that corporate heads do not know which way to turn? The international economy has lost the remarkable stability that served it so well since the Second World War: GATT is in danger, and currency, strictly controlled for so long by the Bretton Woods agreements, has been behaving in an increasingly volatile way. The dollar no longer works as a standard. How to plan one's exports, when all the brokers are nervously looking towards Germany? No one would dare predict how the Japanese or European currencies are likely to evolve.

We need not, however, be pessimistic about the future.

The economic boom persists, but on a different basis. We can see it in countries, in regions that have begun their transition, changed direction, made a genuine readjustment. Prometheus will return. That transitional period we are now experiencing will create the conditions for his reappearance as we adapt to our changed circumstances. The better we understand the current rupture, the better our chances to weather the transition unscathed. And those who reach an understanding earliest will be rewarded with a front seat in Prometheus's next chariot!

3

NO MORE
FORMULAS!

Is management a science? No, just an
assortment of techniques that have
become gospel during the few short years
of abundance and economic growth. Now
these techniques are outmoded; businesses
that insist on adhering to them will disappear.

Great success stories always
result from gambles, brilliant
intuitions that no one had ever dared put into practice.
Schools of management, however, teach the exact opposite.
They show us how to reduce risk in our decision-making, or
provide us with models, taught in the cloistered environment of classrooms or costly seminars.

Whether it be the famous Model T of Henry Ford, Michael
Dell's marketing of computers by correspondence, the
creation of a chain of toy stores called Toys "R" Us, no one
could have foreseen that these products or concepts would
succeed, for they did not correspond to any case studies
taught at Harvard! In general, too, great ideas are conceived
by people who have no master of business administration

degree. Holders of MBAs come along later to manage the outcome, not to make leaps into the unknown.

Management is not a science; it is a discipline, an art. On the basis of experience, it enunciates principles, fixes goals. But in the final analysis, managers find themselves alone with their instincts, and the worldviews they incarnate. This we have forgotten, to our detriment, for the extraordinary economic growth of the last half-century has permitted planning professionals to succeed simply by aping the apparently infallible methods of their predecessors.

THE END OF ARTISANS

When, during the last century, a few years before the discovery of oil, the Frenchman Joseph-Marie Jacquard developed his automatic loom, he had no idea he would be shaking up organized industry the world over. The idea of this technician, who was in no sense a manager, was simply to speed up the work of the weavers. He drew inspiration from the perforated paper strips that make the music in barrel organs. Applied to the looms, it made it possible to automatically create cloth with complex patterns, with the worker who handled the machine needing to know nothing at all about weaving.

The information the artisan once carried around in his head was now found on the perforated strips. The advantages were enormous: an acceleration of the process; uniform quality; a cheaper work force, since it was unskilled and could be replaced at will. Two fifteen-year-old employees could oversee four looms, each of which did the work of nine artisans.

THE BIRTH OF THE MANAGERS

But the most profound change passed unnoticed: that the artisan no longer had control over his own product. More precisely, that the artisan who, up to then, knew his product and its market, gave way to the worker who followed orders. From now on, everything would be run by the manufacturer, the *manager*. He was neither a weaver, nor a merchant. His principal duties were to make the workers work, organize their tasks, plan purchases and sales, and buy new machines that would produce more, more cheaply, thanks to those economies of scale that had not yet been given a name.

To do so, the manager had to surround himself with people who could gather information on markets and in workshops, who could come up with new ways to improve production, make sure the workers were doing their jobs, push them to produce more efficiently. Thus was born the managing executive. He produced nothing, but he looked to the future, planned, organized, controlled.

A few years later, the discovery of oil and the commercial boom that it produced led Rockefeller to conceive of vertical and horizontal integration. One had to expand as quickly as possible to dominate the largest number of new markets, but also had to run the enterprise economically. Planning, organization, and integration did not arise from scientific research but from the gut feeling of entrepreneurs who knew how to profit from a new, predictable environment in which growth itself was possible and predictable. They had found a way to live in symbiosis with that environment.

THE MANAGER WITHOUT A FACE

A smooth-running organization is needed to ensure that a number of people can achieve the goal of producing objects as quickly as possible. Each worker must perform his assigned task in a way that doesn't slow down the others. In such a context, discipline is the watchword, for the aim is not to innovate or improve but to produce rapidly. At the end of the assembly line waits the client: one must deliver the goods to him before a competitor does so.

Here there is no place for individual initiative or creativity. On the contrary, the manager must be certain that everyone does his duty as efficiently as possible. And so it is important to divide up the tasks, and, given the large number of employees and workers, to provide for several hierarchical levels, so that each manager will be responsible for the number of employees he can control effectively.

The success of such a business so relies on its management that one comes to identify them completely: the business is an organization, the organization is a business. This soon became an object of study in and of itself. Sociologists and psychologists hired by schools of management tirelessly researched the ways in which power was exercised in businesses. One among them, Adolf Berle, wrote, in *Power*: "No collective assembly, of whatever class or group, exerts power on its own, nor could it. Another factor is essential: organization." The enterprise is, by definition, a place where power is wielded. And this power takes precedence even over the functions of the entrepreneur. Which led the economist Galbraith to declare, in *The New Industrial State* (1967), that those personalities who laid the groundwork for capitalism's moral authority, in the beginning, had now passed from the scene. "The entrepreneur no longer exists as an individual person in the mature industrial enterprise. . . . the directing force of the enterprise [is] management."

And management was promoting a new worldview: given a growing economy and demand, one must always produce more. More than yesterday, less than tomorrow: next year must always be better than the last. A budget can only increase as the years go by. To meet these objectives, companies required large technical infrastructures, an ever greater number of employees and workers, far-reaching and effective distribution networks. Indeed, starting with a local market, businesses were fated to grow steadily on the national stage, then to export, to create affiliates abroad, and finally, to integrate vertically and horizontally. This view of the world gave rise to a series of principles designed to enable enterprises to flourish in that environment. And as long as the world matched this vision, the principles functioned very well.

THE SCHOOLS GET INVOLVED

All that remained was for the schools to pick apart the formulas of business leaders to derive universal methods and principles. As, by definition, the schools lagged some distance behind the real world, teaching establishments became interested in large enterprises at a point when the entrepreneurs had already been pushed aside. Case studies produced increasingly precise organizational models. Economics, finance, sociology, psychology contributed scientific arguments to these analyses. It seemed that management could be expressed in universal precepts, and we elevated it to the status of a science.

But this was a mistake. In fact, the formulas taught in management schools could only work in the very specific environment of the 20th century. During that period, just as we were constructing a global political and economic order, we had at our disposal more and more abundant and less and less expensive energy. Concurrently, the processing and circulation of information accelerated to a degree that was totally unhoped for and unexpected. We perfected methods and means adapted to this continuous growth, free of hitches or surprises. It was relatively easy because each and all, in a stable universe, drew on comparable data and situations, the same vocabulary, and familiar tools, while applying similar models.

DECEPTIVE CERTAINTIES

Thanks to theorizing based on case studies, the manager was able, perhaps for the first time in history, to cast off his greatest fear: uncertainty. An entrepreneur by definition is a risk-taker, one who dares venture into the unknown. But he tries, of course, to gain control as far as possible over future developments, to reduce uncertainty to a minimum in order to give himself the greatest chance of success. He therefore experiments with all sorts of formulas that he finds trustworthy in varying degrees, and retains those that have proved their worth: that have given results. But all of a sudden, thanks to the great stability at the beginning of the 20th century, he could define parameters that appeared to be universal. His formulas seemed more and more like proven methods. And they were "to organize," "to plan," "to control."

These principles, which to us seemed innate and universal, were only accommodations to specific circumstances. They were invalid when production was in the hands of artisans without surplus energy, and without the means of communication we've known for the last 100 years.

Those precepts may be summarized in a few short sentences. Since our surroundings evolve in a predictable way, let us organize. Since the opportunities to do business and make progress are unlimited, let us plan. Since technology enables us to produce in great volume, let us expand to take advantage of economies of scale. And once more, since we are expanding, let us organize.

Organize, plan, expand: that is what defines a good manager; where ideas are concerned, everything is there. It is assumed that there is an almost perfect symbiosis, both economic and social, between management practice and the environment. There is even a sort of vicious circle: their understanding of the universe encouraged businesses to act in such a way that not only was there a perfect match between, but also a reinforcement of, the managers' vision and the decisions they took. In organizing with expansion in mind, one helped accelerate growth by reinforcing both growth and the urgency to organize.

Prolonged success consolidated this vision, this symbiosis, and from it intellectuals derived formulas that would shape the thinking of generations of businessmen, formulas that would condition their very reflexes.

FORMULA ONE: ECONOMIES OF SCALE

What are they? A natural consequence of the conviction that tomorrow will be better than yesterday. Markets expand indefinitely; the opportunities to do business multiply; we must therefore produce quickly and in great quantity. The results are known in advance: increased sales, a better use of human and material resources, and, therefore, greater profits. And so the first concern of managers is always growth. Small banks think: "Ah! If we were bigger, it would cost us less to run our computers!" In fact they are wrong: their computer system costs them more because they are trying to copy those of the major banks instead of designing a system appropriate to their needs. The myth is deeply rooted that expansion is always the goal. But if you look at the most profitable businesses, you will find that they are almost never among the largest.

Let us take, for example, the ratings of the 100 biggest American corporations in 1992, as set out in *Fortune* magazine. Only one of them was among the most profitable. Surely that proves that size is not a guarantee of economic success. We now see such giants as General Motors subdividing into smaller autonomous units or eliminating their peripheral activities in favour of small specialized companies. No enterprise can attach as much importance to an activity that brings in 5% of its profits as to one that garners it 50%. The first is therefore neglected and operates inefficiently. It would be better by far to entrust it to a firm that could devote 100% of its energies to it.

It is curious how many businesses have overlooked the costs involved in growth, not asking themselves whether these costs would outrun the benefits of economies of scale.

To coordinate the work of three parts factories in two different countries costs much more than to manage one factory under the direct supervision of the owner. In such a case, the merits of geographical diversification and economies of scale are doubtful.

To foresee the fluctuations in money markets everywhere a multinational corporation operates, to create reserves as a hedge against change, to predict the evolution in tastes on three sub-continents, doesn't happen by magic: growth has a cost that can exceed by a large margin the increase in profits it is likely to create.

To communicate with and get agreement from executives of many different nationalities, representing a number of economic, political, and cultural milieus, is also costly. This cost often outstrips the growth in profits, even if there are exceptions. During the 1960s, IBM was able to establish its ascendancy in the field of mainframe computers, thanks to its policy of global expansion, because there existed a market that no one had exploited and which therefore was bound to grow. Since that time, no one has been able to dispute IBM's dominance in that market. Boeing adopted an identical strategy in the field of large passenger airliners. Of course, the success of these two giants inspired admiration and envy on the part of business leaders. Many made the mistake of thinking that this model was good for everyone, in every market, at any time.

But every day history teaches us that this is false. These are unique cases, occurring in periods of extreme economic growth, in new markets, involving corporations with enormous financial resources, ready to sacrifice their profits for many years.

FORMULA TWO: THE LEARNING CURVES

Learning curves have been the bane of many entrepreneurs. They believed, certainly, that economies of scale and growth would require a period of adjustment. Consultants warned them that at first things would be difficult, that costs would be higher than they ought to be. But as time went on and they learned the ropes, everything would get better, and since they were first in line they would come out on top. "You don't see your profits increasing? Don't worry," they were told, "that will come in due course. Look at what IBM and Boeing went through before they began to reap dividends."

But this was not necessarily true. IBM itself learned that lesson in the personal computer market. The presence of competitors already well established in the market rendered useless IBM's financial power, its strength in research and development, its investment in marketing. The economies of scale were an illusion. And IBM eventually had to defer before entrepreneurs that had once seemed insignificant. It had to undertake an operation of massive downsizing: it handed over the manufacturing of microcomputers to another company, under another brand name, and laid off its employees by the tens of thousands. The economies of scale and their corollary, learning curves, had lost their universal status.

In Canada, many examples may be found among those very successful companies that saw Canada as being too small. They crossed the border exporting their methods. They wanted to grow. They encountered problems but persisted. But reality caught up with a vengeance. Culmar, Peoples, Canadian Tire, and Dylex struggled badly overall because of their incursion into the United States.

Let us note in passing that the learning curves provided a rationale for the racking up of enormous debt loads. In effect, since an investment in the means of production only bore fruit later on, it was normal to go into debt while awaiting the hoped-for payoff. Imagine the financial catastrophes, bankruptcies, layoffs, and the ruin of small investors, as managers woke up to the fact that their faith in a prosperous future was unjustified.

FORMULA THREE: THE ORGANIZATION OF PRODUCTION

This formula has been discredited for good. The Second World War introduced American competence to the world, and the West embraced it as a model. A new myth circulated in industrial countries: that the secret of growth lay in organizing production or in the principle of efficiency.

Post-war markets experienced mind-boggling growth: Western Europe was being rebuilt thanks to money provided by the Marshall Plan, while America, with very few debts up to the 1960s, boasted wealth that would have enabled it to grow even without foreign outlets. What was important, therefore, was to manufacture products as efficiently as possible in order to profit from these markets. Harvard and Carnegie built themselves excellent reputations by showing just how to increase effectiveness in production.

Where did that lead us? We forgot about the product. We became so efficient in manufacturing it that we often neglected to ask if it was any good. We had to make it as quickly as possible, in the largest possible quantities. This way of managing corresponded perfectly to the vision of continuous growth: one had to satisfy markets that were ever larger, ever wealthier. The product would always sell — all we had to do was produce it in sufficient numbers.

For production to be efficient, it had to be organized, and scrupulously controlled. Machines set the pace for the employees, requiring economy of movement and as few interruptions as possible. The tasks were therefore divided up, timed, supervised, monitored. A rigid organization took shape, in which a respect for the norms of production took precedence over a concern for the norms of the product. If the product was defective at the end of the production line, it was run once again through the process, which itself was never called into question. Errors were attributed to a faulty application of management directives. They were therefore corrected by an increase in control. But the directives themselves, and the managers, were above suspicion.

We should have looked further. The principle of efficiency focused the enterprise in on itself, on its organization. That was legitimate, but repeated success in doing things right deflected the mind and the imagination from one fundamental question: "Are we doing the right things?"

We had become accustomed to planning, and so to looking ahead. What was important, we thought, in a universe that continues to grow, where business opportunities are legion, was to plan this growth. We must know where we are going, pursue long-term objectives, and not let ourselves be distracted by incidents along the road. With the path clear, we could set ourselves a precise schedule.

The examples of Boeing and IBM would seem to bear out this way of seeing things. If these corporations had not planned long term, they would never have developed the Jumbo Jet or the 360 computer. But that required channelling all their energies into a single project. IBM therefore planned its 360 at the appropriate moment. On the other hand, long-term planning prevented it from seeing how the markets were changing. Others did see: Digital launched its minicomputer in 1965, eleven years before IBM. The Apple II was born in 1977, four years before the IBM PC. Work stations based on Sun Microsystems' RISK technology appeared in 1987, three years before the IBM RS/6000. For the last 20 years, IBM has literally spent all its time chasing the leaders. Only the reputation it built ten years earlier enabled it to survive.

FORMULA FOUR: STRATEGIC PLANNING

Things really took a turn for the worse when, in the 1980s, managers came up with their last formula based on a concept of continuous growth: strategic planning. It made for an interesting contradiction, for it is difficult to imagine how one can devote oneself to planning and strategy at the same time. Planning fine-tunes, as precisely as possible, the entire organization. It influences the coordination of its supplies, its financing, its capital investment, and so on. It therefore requires a specific goal. Strategy, on the other hand, consists in dictating a general approach in pursuit of a goal that's still vague, and poorly defined. It is as we manoeuvre, as we work our way in, that the goal, bit by bit, becomes clear. Either we throw ourselves into planning and decide in advance on the steps we will take, the procedure we will follow, the resources we will require to achieve a specific goal, or we dedicate ourselves to an ongoing clarification of our aims, in response to the shifting parameters of our environment. We cannot do both things at once.

Strategy adapts to the environment; planning imposes its grid on the environment. To combine the two approaches is like trying to hit a moving target with a fixed cannon.

Why on earth did managers go so drastically wrong? Because planning had done so well in a period of rapid economic growth, and they could not bring themselves to renounce it, not having yet come to terms with the fact that economic conditions had changed and that one could no longer control the future. Nevertheless, as they were not blind or stupid, they sensed the world was becoming less stable. And so they had to try for more flexibility, to resort to strategy. The attempt was made to modify an older, outmoded way of operating by superimposing a new one. Unfortunately, the two were mutually exclusive.

DEATH OF A SYMBIOSIS

And so the management style of the '50s and '60s was perfectly suited to the economic, political, and social conditions that began to emerge during the last half of the nineteenth century, and peaked during the 1960s.

The planning of commercial activities was a function of their proliferation. We had to foresee when and how we were going to conquer these new markets. Economies of scale encouraged us to expand. The growth of business required a concomitant growth in organization.

Management principles and the environment therefore

made a coherent whole, an arrangement whereby each element supported all others. But when one of these elements falls by the wayside, everything collapses, and our understanding of the world no longer corresponds to reality. And, indeed, one of these elements, accelerated economic growth, vanished from the scene. As a result, business organization fell on evil days.

This environment of stability, in which we felt so much at ease, boasted two features that we thought were carved in stone: growth and stability. Managers, like other mortals, have great difficulty imagining what they have not experienced. Our memory goes back no more than a generation. And when our universe is disrupted, we lose all the reference points we thought were immutable. It's as though the controls that we had used to navigate the future were taken out of our hands. And so we grope for new ones, trying to develop other ways of controlling our environment. In the meantime, we watch while businesses we thought were so stable and powerful as to be eternal drop from sight. Businesses are not eternal; they last only as long as they are in harmony with their surroundings.

We can sum up the philosophy of management in the 20th century with a simple image. The prospect of endless progress led business to set for itself ever more ambitious goals. We were all convinced that the summit of Everest was accessible and that the means to attain it were known. We refined them, but they called for systemization, planning. Conquering Everest was a project whose realization was complex, but computable. We had to choose the teams, divide the ascent into stages, make sure there were enough porters for equipment and food, so that at the end of the climb a select group would reach the top. The conquest of Everest, sustained growth, the means to succeed, planning and control, all were interdependent. But if there were a breakdown, if sustained growth were to disappear, we would not only have to alter our approach, but to define what new goal was now appropriate.

Next we will try to imagine our environment in the coming century, and how we will be able to adapt to it.

4

HOW ORGANIZATIONS IMPLODE

Hypertrophied, bloated with middle-level management, traditional organizations are like bodies whose limbs send no message to the brain.

"A business will go nowhere if some parts of it are turning right, and others left." The author of this succinct analysis is not just anyone, but Yoshikazu Hanawa, vice-president of Nissan Motors. In less colourful terms: in an organization you need one boss and one only, and everyone else must fall into step like a well-oiled machine, or, if you prefer, a disciplined army.

Now no one can supervise, alone, the functioning of a corporation made up of many divisions, located in several different places, manufacturing a number of products. The head office can only perform this miracle by dividing the company into numerous sub-entities that are given specific tasks: marketing, production, accounting, sales, service, and so on. This is the reason for specialization in the workplace. At the top of the hierarchical pyramid, the president has a number of vice-presidents accountable to him. Each is responsible for one type of business activity. They set their course in accordance with the president's wishes, which are carried out by a cohort of third-level managers, and so on down the pyramid to an employee who humbly obeys orders that reach him from a source to which he never has access and whose intentions and motivations he cannot know. If such employees are responsible for production, they have no knowledge of their clients, either, for this is the domain of marketing. And if the employee is in marketing, he is ignorant of the constraints and the potential of the system of production. Totally in the dark, compliers comply, without seeking to understand. They are therefore difficult to motivate. For that, business psychologists develop wage policies, fringe benefits, and strategies that will encourage a feeling of belonging. "Our business is one big family," they have owners say, blithely indifferent to the meaninglessness of their words.

The employees, the workers, are therefore thrust into an organization of which they know practically nothing, and for which they can show no initiative. Furthermore, they are instructed not to show any initiative, because that might slow down production!

THE MILITARIZATION OF ORGANIZATIONS

Henry Ford gave an excellent account of the simplification of tasks when he maintained that, out of the 7,882 operations needed to assemble a Model T, "949 were classified as heavy work requiring strong, able-bodied, and practically physically perfect men; 3,338 required men of ordinary physical develop-ment and strength. The remaining 3,595 jobs were disclosed as requiring no physical exertion and could be performed by the slightest, weakest sort of men. . . . 670 could be filled by legless men, 2,637 by one-legged men, 2 by armless men, 715 by one-armed men, and 10 by blind men."

Since the worker no longer thinks, he no longer passes on information to management. That simplifies things: information only has to flow downwards. The information is never questioned, there being no thinking done in the lower echelons, and so management consists only in giving orders. The organization becomes militarized. As in an army, the generals speak to majors, who speak to corporals, who speak to the troops.

This system works perfectly well in a world where the product must be very standardized, or where models change very little. We have seen this earlier on, where the tastes of consumers are simple, and known, and cost is an important factor. There is no reason to create avenues of communication from the bottom up, which would only slow down the process, increase expenses, reduce efficiency.

THE DOMINANCE OF POWER

When the board of General Motors, the biggest manufacturer of automobiles in the world, decided to change its direction radically, it enlisted the services of a new board chairman, John Smale, who had done wonders at Procter & Gamble, boosting the sales of cosmetic products. This had nothing to do with automobiles. All the board wanted was someone who could run a business, or at least choose those who would be able to do so. The result was a massive reorganization of GM, with the corporation's new guard in the driver's seat and everything orchestrated by the board under Smale's direction.

IBM's actions were even more telling. There again, an outside administrator, the former president of Johnson & Johnson, offered the direction of IBM to the president of RJR Nabisco, Louis Gerstner. He was named following the biggest leveraged buyout in history. According to rumours, he knew almost nothing about technology, and there he was at the head of a corporation that had led the world in that field for 40 years. He was regarded as an "organizer," a kind of surgeon for business culture.

Businesses had become *organizations* in which the priority was to marshal all human resources (people were now only resources, comparable to oil, electricity, or machinery). Dominance and authority had become so crucial that they were as important as the company's reason for being. Professional managers could move from a manufacturer of perfumes and soap to one that assembled automobiles, for no one required that they know how to stuff cereal into boxes, or put scooters together. They were asked to organize, to make sure no one turned right while everyone else was turning left, in the words, again, of Yoshikazu Hanawa.

THE INVERTED PYRAMID

Traditional organization is military, with the important people at the top. Salaries are determined by one's position in the hierarchy. To reward an employee, one must promote him. As long as the business is growing, there is no problem: one adds rungs to the ladder, for there are always more employees to supervise, more tasks to accomplish. Even when growth stops, or slows down, we continue to add new steps, and to enlarge the pyramid. Administration becomes more and more all-consuming. Managers, so as not to feel superfluous, and to justify their existence, look for things to do. They begin to think, to hold meetings, and to make plans (preferably "strategic" ones). And their plans concern their own jobs or principal activities. Production, proportionately, comes to involve fewer and fewer people. The pyramid is inverted: the thinking head grows larger than the base that produces and sells.

Such ingrown organization caused huge losses in productivity that no one wants to acknowledge even though it is plain to see. During the 1980s, in the United States, the number of workers grew by 2% while that of office employees increased by 33%. During the same period, average production grew by 30%; but while worker productivity jumped 28%, that of office employees went down 3%.

Growth in the United States would have been identical to that in the rest of the world, but the presence of twice the number of office employees to workers cancelled out the entire gain in productivity.

The teaching of management naturally followed the trends and gave priority to reflection and thought. Businesses were flooded with people with a gift for thinking, an aptitude for analysis, the capacity to fill out detailed reports, to establish guidelines . . . But how many among them gave any thought to how their decisions would be applied? How many bothered to keep up to date on changes in technology that would facilitate manufacturing? How many, even, were able to make decisions? Very few. For 100 people involved in planning, ten are qualified to make decisions and only one to make the decisions stick and see that they show results.

We take performance for granted, and we dream of automating it. Such an attitude on the part of business is extremely self-centred: the organization is concerned for itself rather than the outside world and rather than the client.

Management for management's sake has, notoriously, cancelled out all the benefits gained from the computerization of accounting. Accounting was computerized in the U.S. between 1978 and 1985. As a result, production increased by 16%. But at the same time, the number of accountants grew by 30%, from 1 million to 1.3 million. What happened? Computers made it possible to calculate faster, and the accountants took advantage of this to beef up their accounting. Accounts that had been updated every three months, now were revised every day. A whole new class of data that could not be computed before was now available on demand. Did that make for better management? No one knows. What is certain is that the pyramid swelled and the owner could better control his staff and shore up the military side of his enterprise. The client, on the other hand, did not benefit at all.

What's more, with the division of labour, the owner had the impression this information cost him nothing, since the expense was charged not to his own budget but to that of his subordinates. The latter did not object to providing the information or ask themselves if it served any purpose: given the military structure, they did what was asked of them.

Old ways of management die hard. Rather than change them, we always try to make do as best we can.

BUSINESS BEFOGGED

At the top of the pyramid, managers found it harder and harder to know where they stood, in a tentacular organization whose purpose was increasingly obscure. They therefore enlisted the services of a personnel adviser. This individual had nothing to do with the business. His responsibility was to synthesize what went on in one part of the organization, to extract information from that data, and to communicate it in bits and pieces to upper management, which, from out of the fog, would try to make good decisions.

Attempts were made not to promote worthy employees; motivational bonuses were introduced, in order to maintain them at their current level. This slowed the pyramid's growth, but did not stop it.

When it became obvious there were lessons to be learned

from the employees on the floor, "quality circles" became fashionable. But the results were minimal, because these groups, in which the workers were asked for their input, were assimilated into the old order; the groups' reports were lost in the administrative shuffle of paper.

High-level thinking continued to prevail over production lower down in the organization. The decision-makers in the executive suites, with full confidence in their military system, took it for granted that their decisions would be carried out. But the environment was no longer the same: technology had changed and workers had changed, without anyone upstairs really having noticed. The managers were losing grasp of their surroundings.

THE IMPLOSIVE MATRIX

The organization, in its last stage, has been transformed into an imposing administrative pyramid. This type of structure has been so dominant, for decades, that businesses are now referred to as organizations: no distinction is made between the business and the way in which it is managed. By structuring businesses in terms of their different operations, we have separated areas of expertise into hermetic compartments.

No one, any longer, has an overview of the market, the products, the manufacturing. Under such circumstances, who in the corporation can call into question its overall performance? We have, quite naturally, come to a point where business has been divided into its operational components. It is the logical consequence of division of labour. Each manager, perfectly isolated, is committed to his own department, his own unit.

Imagine a business that manufactures computers. It has a small division that helps wholesalers and retailers finance their inventory. This division has nothing to do with the company's true purpose; it is only a byproduct involved in commercialization. How is the director of this financial department going to behave? He will try to expand his program, will work to open up new markets, will dream of offering credit to individuals. His efforts on behalf of the financing division will bloat it out of proportion to the business, which was not designed to perform this function.

No one knows where the ambitions of the financing director may lead. In his enthusiasm, he will try to persuade the head office to back him up. But no one at head office really knows anything about financing, since the purpose of the business is to design and manufacture computers. It is difficult, therefore, to refute the arguments of the financing director, since he's the only one who is competent in that field. The risk is great, then, that a good part of the business's resources will be diverted from manufacturing to his department. He will be gratified that his ideas have been taken seriously and will continue to pursue his strategy of growth. He will proceed with such fervour that head office will leave him in peace until the day the realization dawns that the company's investments in manufacturing are inadequate, and that businesses which specialize in the field of financing are far outclassing the initiatives of our dynamic director.

The only recourse, far too late, is to seek a buyer for the financing division. The cost will be high, since the decision was taken only once the error became so flagrant that it could not be denied. Not only did the division siphon off energies in the wrong direction, but employees will now be laid off who had acquired real skills. Divided internally by task, then by operation, the organization evolved into an implosive matrix, programmed for its own dismemberment.

THE ADVANTAGES OF
DISMEMBERMENT

This dismemberment is actually beneficial. It puts an end to the squandering of vital energy by outsized organizations. In this regard, consider two giant corporations. The first, AT&T, was dismantled by judicial order in 1982. The second, IBM, remained intact. In 1992, we were able to see the results of the two policies. Since 1982, the Baby Bells, those companies born from the fragmentation of AT&T, grew, overall, by 279%. IBM grew 66%. The same year, IBM decided to restructure, and form ten smaller companies. First the Baby Bells, then the Baby Blues . . . The management model for giant organizations is now extinct.

5

FROM ORDER
TO CHAOS

*The Industrial Revolution triggered an
extraordinarily swift mutation in the economic
and social environment of industrialized
countries. We did not foresee that the rapid growth
stability brought in its wake would plunge
us back into disorder when it disappeared.
We are now faced with chaos.*

Ways of life have probably never been disrupted so rapidly as they have since the end of the nineteenth century. In developed countries, life expectancy almost doubled in 30 years. Growth, which stood at 0.79% during the nineteenth century, has increased to almost 1.7% since the 1950s.

We forget too easily that, among the people who will read this book, some no doubt will remember when electricity was first connected and automobiles first appeared in their village and will recall the earliest radio stations and the direct transmission of the astronauts' first steps on the moon. Those who once lit the wood stove in the morning to heat the house now only have to turn a dial to keep the temperature of their apartment at 20 degrees. In one century, distances have changed their meaning. Only 100 years ago, the invention of the bicycle caused a furor in Paris because of its speed! It was only in 1903 that the first airplane powered by an internal combustion engine flew a distance of 300 metres.

WE ARE NO LONGER CREATING ECONOMIC VALUE

The phenomenal changes sparked by the Industrial Revolution resulted almost immediately in the growth of economic value. The transformation of iron ore into an automobile enriched many more people than its transformation into a fireplace poker. This evolution inspired the hope that the standard of living would improve. Of course, there were victims: those who lost their jobs as a result of automation, or those who saw the products they manufactured become outmoded. But even here society produced enough wealth to take measures that would help overcome the difficulties caused by industrial activity. Unemployment insurance, health care programs, guaranteed minimum wage, free schooling to the university level, were all 20th-century innovations that only the creation of economic value could have made possible. Economic growth and the resulting prosperity gave rise to great social and political stability.

But the pace has slowed considerably. Certainly, technological advances occur, but at nowhere near the rate that sustained us for a century. The current fine-tuning of cars, computers, airplanes, or the banking system will not bring about the economic and social revolutions to which we became accustomed during the first half of the century. Inevitably, the creation of value has dropped off.

The most ordinary automobile we now manufacture would have been a luxury car immediately after the Second World War. In fact, at that time, we probably would have been unable to make it. Its price would have been prohibitive. Now its value is insignificant, not even equal to the minimum annual wage. We need hardly mention computers, which in the 1950s were virtually the stuff of science fiction. We now find them everywhere in all kinds of offices, and they'll soon be in most homes and many even in cheap toys. Their value has plummeted.

We did not realize that the marked economic growth that had stabilized our environment would throw us into disarray once it came to an end. To explain this phenomenon, let us think of a river. If its current is strong, it will flow at a steady rate, even if its bed is covered with stones. It would be very easy to predict the speed and direction of a leaf floating on the surface. On the other hand, as the current weakens, the flow is increasingly disturbed. At first there are a few whirlpools here and there, not so serious as to prevent us from predicting the course the leaf will follow. But bit by bit the water seethes and becomes chaotic; the river is transformed. No one, any more, can chart the progress of an object being carried along.

This is what we are experiencing now. The slowing of the economy and a slump in added value have thrown our society into general confusion. This is evident, notably, in the evolution of our major currencies: for decades, their value only fluctuated about 1%; now they can move 5% within a week, and 50% in a year.

COMPETITION BECOMES RUINOUS

When growth ceases, competition, always there like reefs beneath the water, becomes extremely dangerous, to the point of being ruinous. Chaos means instability. The smallest incident, however banal, can create unexpected upheavals. You have doubtless heard of the butterfly effect: theoretically, a simple fluttering of butterfly wings could, step by step, trigger·a typhoon on the other side of the planet.

In a balanced system, one in which constant forces are operating in equilibrium, a fluttering of wings cannot conceivably result in a cataclysm. But in a universe where the major lines of force have been fragmented and chaos reigns, no one any longer can predict what events will or will not have a significant effect. Our socioeconomic universe is now so vulnerable that a seemingly minor variant can have enormous consequences. A tiny sect can destabilize a sub-continent. A Native member of the legislature in Manitoba can scuttle Canada's constitutional reform. An obscure student, a certain Michael Dell, can invent a new sales technique for personal computers that will disrupt the development plans of the world's corporate giants in the field.

Long-term planning is now impossible, for one can be sure that a competitor will soon come up with a new way to respond to the client's needs, whether it be a novel manufacturing process, a diversification in his stock, a new method of financing, a partnership with another business . . . Anything is possible. Competition has become ruinous.

THE POLITICIANS AT A LOSS

The political world is in comparable disarray. We only have to look, for example, at the fragmentation of the Balkan states into a number of ethnic groups impossible to reconcile, or confrontation in Arab countries between fundamentalists and progressives. All these conflicts show that our political systems are on the verge of collapse, challenged as they are by an emerging individualism that has made enormous headway since the capitalist view of the world prevailed over its communist opposition.

The 20th century has been a laboratory for two ideas: one

gave society precedence over the individual, and the other valued the individual over society. Communism wanted to relieve man of life's hardships: the state would find jobs for all its citizens, provide them with a salary, an apartment, and plan their careers. All responsibility was collective. This approach led to the creation of a bureaucratic and centralized state.

By contrast, capitalism consciously rejected a monolithic political organization and favoured pluralism, putting the emphasis on the individual. According to this system, at least in theory, everyone had the right to a fair wage for his work.

Today the vast majority of people are convinced that the second option was the right one. The primacy of the individual is recognized the world over: the individual is valued and can at last give expression to a variety of sexual preferences, ethnicities, culinary practices, and political systems. That is the reason, no doubt, that tastes have become so intense and so ephemeral.

Given these tendencies, centralist and prescriptive policies are coming apart at the seams. The great superstructures (the United Nations, the European Community, etc.) are being called into question. Cities and regions want more and more to control their own destinies, to provide their own solutions to specific problems. Traditional politics no longer gives the results it once did. New ways will have to be found to govern nations.

CAPITALISM IN METAMORPHOSIS

The chaotic nature of our environment need not be seen in a negative light. By forcing us to adapt, constantly, to a changing world, chaos provides a stimulus for our creativity. There, however, is the rub. North American business has always excelled in organization and mass production, but creativity has been its Achilles heel.

Business knows how to produce identical objects in great profusion, while the new environment requires the flexible, imaginative production of personalized articles and services. Industry must therefore try to shorten the reaction time of its organization, to restrict the number of hierarchical levels, to bring clients and brainstormers together in order to respond quickly to, or anticipate, new needs.

Capitalism had endorsed the primacy of the individual, but above all of the individual as entrepreneur. A hero of American culture, the entrepreneur was inclined to organize everything in terms of himself and in conformity with his ideas, to the detriment of other players in the business. Psychologists called in to teach at management schools understood that very well, because they came from quite a different milieu. That is the reason courses in industrial psychology place so much emphasis on the expression of power and authority in the enterprise. The centralized and hierarchical organization of a company is a product of the way power is wielded.

The Bombardier group, a world leader in transportation equipment from Ski-Doos to EuroTunnel cars, understood that the new environment now demands a radical change in direction: that of respecting individuals at all levels of the business, letting them express themselves creatively and allowing competent people to make decisions at their level which are more effective, appropriate, and rapid. The end of bureaucratization in business is at hand.

A company's response to the rise of individualism in society must include greater respect for those individuals who make up the population of that company. The approach is perfectly coherent. Managers must first understand the importance of the people within their walls, but then also beyond them, for what they've lost sight of is whom they are there to serve, the client (just as communism forgot *its* purpose, the well-being of its citizens). Today we see the consequences.

Why was capitalism able to adapt, while communism foundered? Because capitalism was never a system of thought. There is no bible of capitalism. It was simply born from the conjunction of democracy and the individual's freeing of himself from the sovereign's yoke. People were told they had the right to the fruits of their labour, whereas before they worked and received from their lord whatever he chose to grant them. We have changed all that, although little by little the state has once more become, through the taxes it levies, a usurper and a centralizing force.

The strength of capitalism is that it is not founded in doctrine, and so it can adapt without anyone accusing it of heresy or reformism. That is what has enabled it to put down roots, in different guises, in every world economy, even those that condemned it and opposed it most intensely.

THE LAW OF THE MARKETS

The markets have always been in control, and capitalism has only adapted to them. Sometimes this adaptation has had unexpected consequences, such as the globalization of markets that nobody wanted. Any idea, any technology, any invention that appears anywhere in the world can now instantly and radically alter the conditions in a local market. From now on, long-term planning has no meaning, and the entrepreneur must quickly adapt to each change by drawing on all possible resources available to his enterprise, principally the capability, creativity, and expertise of his employees.

The problems the entrepreneur must resolve will not only be organizational in nature, but will often be technological and related to methods of production. The focus will therefore shift from the head office to the factories and workshops where creativity will become a prized possession. Authority will not mean telling people what they ought to do, but mobilizing workers so they themselves can make the best decisions.

CHAOS, THE HOPE OF THE NEW ORDER

Chaos carries within it the seeds of another kind of organization, one in which apparently random movements ultimately create lines of force that bring about a new cohesion. The impetuous torrent eventually orders the stones strewn in its bed, and bit by bit regulates its flow. Mathematicians and physicists are very interested in this phenomenon. They have observed, for example, that within the enormous chaos of the planet Mars, there exists an extremely stable whirlwind, one that has been there for ages. Researchers have artificially re-created an atmosphere much like that of Mars, subject to turbulence that is just as unpredictable. To their astonishment, two whirlwinds rapidly formed, gradually coming together to form one that was very stable. Chaos ultimately created a new order.

Let us take another example, this one closer to the world of management. The International Monetary Fund was created largely to stabilize the money market. We now know with certainty, just as was suspected at the time of the Bretton Woods agreements, that the Depression of the 1930s was amplified and prolonged by protectionist policies. These measures included devaluations the industrial nations imposed on themselves in order to gain a "competitive advantage." International trade, as a result, was disrupted. The stabilizing of exchange rates restored business confidence and encouraged imports and exports free of the enormous financial risks that can result from sudden fluctuations in the value of money.

This order had its day, but it was replaced by a new order, that of flexible exchange rates. We let currencies fluctuate, but there is no longer any disorder. The chaos of fluctuation has created a new order much more durable, flexible, and supple than the rigidity of exchange parity. Today an exporter can guarantee his sales price by buying currency even before he ships the merchandise. Someone on the financial market will run the risk for him. The price to be paid is much less severe than that of maintaining artificial parity or that of a brutal devaluation, such as occurred in 1992 when the lira and the pound sterling withdrew from the European monetary system, then known as the "monetary snake."

This poor snake, precursor to a common European currency, was designed to re-establish order and stability. Forced to perform impossible convolutions, it gave rise to even greater disorder. Order is born from chaos; its strength derives from its being a child of circumstance. Disorder is what comes of an imposed order.

6

THE CUSTOMERS
ARE CRAZY

*It is no longer the product that is important, but how
to sell it. New incarnations of old products are so
numerous that consumers constantly change their
minds. Their tastes have become unpredictable and
extravagant, intense and ephemeral.*

When the phonograph was invented, it took several decades before the market was saturated, and the same was true of the telephone, radio, television, automatic washer and dryer. For the designers of new products, there was no problem: the market was so vast that with good publicity campaigns, and reasonably adequate products, sales were assured. Once the market was saturated, a date relatively easy to forecast, it became important to prepare another product. As long as markets were expanding, creativity and manufacturing could be planned. That's the producer's side of the story.

The consumer, for his part, with his buying power continuing to grow, saw new products appear each year and bought them to enhance his quality of life.

In the early stages of their commercialization, there was

not much to choose between one product and another: you owned a dishwasher or you didn't, you had a VCR or you did not. But when the product became mature, the struggle between manufacturers was to see who could come up with additional features that would tempt the consumer to renew his purchase earlier than intended, and more important still, to select that product rather than the competitor's.

The automobile was without doubt one of the first products of mass consumption to exemplify this phenomenon. Ford had achieved success with its black Model T's. Customers were delighted to be able to buy a car that was not too expensive: the important thing was to have a car. But once the market was saturated, Ford ran into trouble when GM, aware of how competition was changing, launched a variety of models. The customer now wanted a model that would distinguish him from his neighbour. Up to the beginning of the 1970s, however, most products remained very simple and most consumers remained very conservative. The telephone was there to make telephone calls, the radio for listening to programs, the alarm clock to wake one up in the morning. If they performed the tasks for which they had been designed, all was well.

FROM USEFULNESS TO PLEASURE

Then growth prospects diminished considerably. To be more exact, we had exhausted the possibilities of these new products. Markets no longer expanded, and no more inventions emerged from the technical knowledge at our disposal. We could, of course, continue to refine the old inventions, but there was little hope of discovering, in the immediate future, a radical way to transform our lives. One day Prometheus would return, but in the meantime we had to make do.

In the short term, the best we could hope for was to

perfect what we already had. The vinyl record was replaced by the compact disc, television became coloured, air-conditioning and anti-lock brakes were installed in automobiles, but no revolutionary inventions appeared on the scene. Here, as well, endless progress had come to an end. Yes, a great discovery lies in wait, but it will be "a surprise," and off the beaten path.

As a consequence, the buyer is left splitting hairs: should I choose the coffeemaker that tells the time, or the one that's calcium resistant? The question for the consumer is no longer "What does this product do?" It is "Which one will give me the most pleasure?" We do not buy a computer because it computes well and quickly, but because it is thin and light. We select an alarm clock because it plays music; a stereo system because it has a remote.

Tom Peters goes so far as to say that products no longer exist, that substance no longer counts. This is the age of fashion, that is to say of style, packaging, appearance, first impressions, salescraft, colour.

In Japan, Toyota has a team of researchers whose task it is to design dashboard controls that are pleasing to use. At Renault, the sound of car doors closing is analysed and adjusted so as to create an impression appropriate to the model. AEG, of the Mercedes group, manufactures clothes dryers that measure the laundry's humidity, so as to determine the intensity and duration of the cycle.

A RAGE FOR NOVELTY

The lives of designers, manufacturers, and retailers of consumer products have become veritable nightmares. Running shoes are no longer white or black, they are stream-lined, ergonomic, moulded, inflatable . . . Who knows what will come next? No one can predict what a competitor will pull out of his hat to attract a buyer. Or whether this novelty will really entice customers. The lifespan of a product has become impossible to forecast. To avoid seeing his product line become outmoded, each manufacturer must continually redesign his models, which of course shortens the life of those now on the shelf.

Manufacturers and consumers have therefore lost their peace of mind. The manufacturer must constantly come up with new ideas and set them in motion before knowing if they will give the desired results. Buyers, for their part, are assailed by an ever-growing choice of models, without knowing if they will be obsolete as soon as they are purchased — or earlier.

Take a stroll through the main floor of a department store, where cosmetics are usually on display. Try to count the number of lipsticks on sale: it boggles the mind! There are hues for morning, noon, formal evenings, intimate soirées . . . and they change from month to month, from region to region. In 1992, Avon opted to increase the number of lipstick shades it offered to 100. And in order to respond instantly to the needs of its clients, it decided to turn them out in batches of 500. Each series would be produced in ten minutes so that the manufacturing process would be as flexible as possible. In order to meet these objectives, the factory floor had to be completely transformed, to allow for smaller machines, and above all, for machines that could be easily retooled for a new line: production had to conform to the same rhythm as the changing tastes of consumers.

The Japanese company Panasonic Cycle has taken flexibility to an extreme. One can order bicycles to measure that are assembled in Japan and delivered within two weeks. Mass production is dead, or at the very least is on its last legs.

An environment characterized by predictability, along

with stable tastes and buying preferences, has given way to one marked by unpredictability and a kind of frenzy. Gratification has to be immediate, and technology, however omnipresent, no longer guarantees a sale. A striking example is the publicity campaign launched by the Apple computer company. Instead of taking on the products of its competitors, it went after a product of Microsoft. This company does not, however, produce computers, but programs that make them easy to use.

The battle between computers, therefore, is no longer conducted in terms of power, rapidity, or durability: it is immediate pleasure that takes priority. In the same field, Dell owes its growth, which has been stupendous, to the fact that one can buy a computer by telephone, receive it within a week, and simply plug it in and have it up and running. No need even to visit a store. The product's greatest attraction is that it arrives on its own, a purchase that is effortless and trouble-free. It is no longer the product that counts, but the way it is sold.

Customers are inclined to shift loyalties depending on the features offered by new products. It's no longer enough for designers to determine their needs; they must anticipate them by inventing novelties . . . and praying they will bring pleasure and satisfaction. Creativity is now of primary importance both in design and in sales, all of which makes life very complicated indeed.

THE FAILURE OF FORESIGHT

During the 1960s and '70s, we were inundated with books inquiring into the future. Now, however, prognostication has ground to a halt. That's to be expected; to have any chance of success in this field, one must live in a predictable universe. Up to the present, our environment was complicated, certainly, but we could still break it down into its components, study them, and try to imagine how they would work once they were put back together. But now we have come to realize that we live in a complex world. Even if we manage to take it apart and get to know all its elements, we cannot foretell what the overall picture will be. Each part reacts with all the others and alters them constantly. For decades, economics and sociology helped us break down the world of business into finite elements we thought we could analyse independently of each other. With some skill in synthesis, one could fashion a global view of business and society, and project it into the future with a fair degree of accuracy. But as of now, it's the system as a whole we must comprehend. Looking at the details has lost a great deal of its usefulness. Today the photographer needs a wide-angle, rather than a telephoto, lens.

Let's take a look at the image of Hervé Serieyx. In the past we encountered difficulties in economics, business, politics, but we had a pretty good idea of the laws that governed them. We could analyse the problems and resolve them. Things were complicated, but the complications were limited and everything was understood, a bit like in a nuclear reactor, whose construction and operation obey known laws. But today is the age of complexity. Instead of a nuclear reactor, we have a plate of spaghetti where all the strands are tangled up in an ungainly snarl. If we make any changes to what is on the plate, it becomes impossible to reconstitute what was there before. The keys and codes that worked in the past cannot possibly cope with this new order of things.

Given this uncertain future, we must learn not to prophesy but to equip ourselves so we can react and evolve along with the system. We must understand it not from the outside, but from within, just as the captain of a small boat caught in a storm must react each moment to the shifting winds, to the direction and shape of the waves even as they form. Neither the course we set, nor our conduct at the wheel, are as predictable as they were when the sea was calm. In the middle of the storm, the captain must deal with it moment by moment: his survival depends on it. It is no longer the conquest of Everest that lies before us, but the navigation of a storm.

WE HAVE BEGAT COMPLEXITY

The manager is in the same situation as the captain in the storm: his universe is random, uncertain. But it is he and his colleagues the world over who have created this situation. Constantly trying to reduce costs while appending new features to old products, they have had to manipulate all facets of the business at the same time: the organization of production, research and development, publicity, the company's image in the eyes of the investors, methods of financing, new materials. All these elements interact: cost reduction and employee motivation are not always compatible, nor are cuts in the profit margin and an enhanced corporate image for the investors. The crux of the problem is that all the competitors in the world are going through the same process and perhaps will succeed better than we, coming up with solutions that will render our response, which was valid yesterday, inadequate tomorrow. Business processes are being re-examined in their totality, opposing complexity to formerly programmed and structured behaviour.

Consider someone groping for a switch in the dark. If he is in a standard house, from the end of the 1940s, it won't take much thought before he finds it, because buildings of that vintage were all equipped according to a simple and consistent pattern. But if he is in a modern apartment, his task is much more complicated, because today every architect strives to do something new, to put the switches in more convenient spots, to alter their design and their way of functioning, even to camouflage them. Thinking is pointless, he's got to grope.

And thus the fundamental point of this book, captured by the image of the captain buffeted by the storm. He acts and thinks at the same time as he reacts to an unpredictable environment. He can still hear the searchlight's foghorn, but he cannot see it.

7

CREATIVITY AND INITIATIVE

Planning has become an enemy to be avoided, for it can only slow our adjustment to changing conditions. First introduced so that we might better respond to an environment characterized by growth and stability, it has become a handicap in a world where competition gives rise to uncertain and unforeseeable consequences. It must give way to creativity, the source of initiative. While planning turns business in on itself and centralizes it, creativity redirects business towards the customer and decentralizes it.

No longer can we predict what our customers will desire tomorrow; we cannot foresee what accounting framework, what financial arrangements, what strategies our competitors will devise to enhance their profitability and efficiency, to diversify their operations. The strength of business now resides in creativity. Creativity cannot be planned, it can only be encouraged and promoted. It requires imagination, trial and error, doubling back, intuition, flair, luck, experience. It is diametrically opposed to planning.

FROM POWER LOANED
TO POWER SHARED

As discussed earlier, managers must shift from planning to strategy, for the present environment makes it difficult to see into the future, to structure, to organize. That means they must react on a daily basis to unforeseen occurrences, to new situations. But they were not trained for that. The 20th century provided them with a number of tools that could have facilitated creative and flexible management; but these tools proved to be counterproductive because instead of being used to stimulate creativity, they were pressed into the service of ever more control.

So it was with computer science. In his book *The Twilight of Sovereignty*, Walter Wriston, former president of Citicorp, emphasizes that the cost of one unit of information, the famous *bit*, was reduced by a factor of 1,000 in 25 years. Management used this new tool to control production, bureaucracy, sales. Their dream was to supervise every employee all the time. But in fact it was the employees who benefitted, by reclaiming a small part of the power that had been refused them. In 1993 the large mainframes represented only 1% of all computers.

In businesses at present, it is often young employees without status who teach their superiors about the remarkable resources of the microcomputer. Most often, their suggestions are not followed up, because the managers have not yet learned that information can and must be shared. It is no longer Big Brother who controls the employees, but the employees who control Big Brother!

This resistance on the part of traditional managers to the sharing of information is reflected in the underuse of the microcomputer's potential in many offices. Databases are used for little more than mailing lists. And so information continues to lie dormant in the managers' drawers. The results are clear: employees are perfectly aware to what degree their expertise, their capacity to make use of information, is ignored.

But it could not be otherwise in a centralized structure. Information and our enhanced ability to process it require an emphasis on an increasingly refined grasp of tiny details. As anyone may have in his possession data more and more specific to certain groups of clients, to regions and sub-regions, the centralization of information tends to undercut its usefulness. Those who make good use of micro-economic data will have a clear advantage, since they will have the tools they can apply to specific conditions.

That indeed is where competition, driven by the expanding power of information, is leading. The margin of error allowing us to satisfy a client is greatly diminished. No more clothes with predetermined sizes, no more all-purpose products, no more standard approaches to the public. Now we must match skill with the growing distinctiveness customers have already begun to exploit.

Fortunately, bit by bit, managers are learning to share information and encourage creativity at all levels of the business. The movement is already under way. Aware that computers are responsible for an excessive bloating of organizations, some companies have begun to entrust their computer processing to specialized firms.

We are, then, in transition between an integrated structure for business and one that is decentralized. The role of the manager is no longer to control everything but to share out power according to the capabilities of each, inside or outside the enterprise.

LONG LIVE DISORGANIZATION

Engineers themselves have no choice but to second-guess their way of working. Let us take the case of a company called on to design a railway car. Twenty years ago, the project's budget would have been calculated at head office, for its needs would have been known: the required amount of metal pipes, square metres of sheathing, springs, and bolts. There were only a few simple decisions to be made: would one use steel or aluminum for the seat frames, cloth or plastic for the upholstery, and how much distance would one allow between each seat? With these few simple decisions, it was possible to organize an entire production.

Now, everything is different. The inside of the car must be conceived as a whole. The seat can have an effect on the rigidity of the carrier. A single piece can serve as the seat's frame, the wall of the car, and the baggage rack. Given the functions each component has to perform, the designer must seek out an appropriate material. In the past, he had a choice of three or four types of steel, all well known. Today, there are thousands of composites. He may choose none of them, but instead develop a new one in order to achieve the results he wants: the weight, the resistance, a pleasing appearance.

It is not the choice of forms, colours, or materials that makes things difficult. Because he must contend with constraints that go far beyond the act of sitting down, the designer of a seat is faced with a very complex task. He must take into account the nature and rigidity of the walls, the type of undercarriage, ergonomics, aesthetics, resistance, and passive security. Decision-making, coordination of the work at hand, must of necessity be carried out by an interdisciplinary team that can weigh in the balance all aspects of the problem.

If they want to keep control of their business, managers

will have to become specialists in design, as the Japanese understood 30 years ago. Given technological chaos, and the need to respond at once to customers' shifting demands, designers, and those responsible for production, must come up with original, economical ideas, fast enough to satisfy, if not anticipate their clients' needs. We can no longer know beforehand where new ideas may originate. In the marketing team that senses the changing tastes of consumers? In the production team that discovers a new technical application to enhance the appeal of a product? Initiative must be delegated and shared at different levels of the business, for all of technology is known and can be applied anywhere in the world. What separates winners from losers is not their technology. It is the way technology is used, and how products are presented.

We must, then, disorganize, give up our old habits, go prospecting for new ideas, as we no longer know from what source they may emerge. We have seen the last of planning, hierarchical organization, employees waiting around for directives. It is not enough any more to adapt to change, we must now get the jump on it, for change is a direct result of competition. What counts is who, first, will have the best idea: a new process, a new colour, a new presentation, a new service.

It's impossible to plan creativity, to foresee disorder. To survive, companies are going to have to conceive new methods, to apply new precepts. As one observer of management has put it, the prerequisite to creativity is rethinking, and the fostering of a *habit* of rethinking.

WINNING OVER OLD CLIENTS

Since customers' tastes are changing, since markets are no longer expanding, we must now organize ourselves to determine what consumers want. The consumer we know best is our current customer; he is therefore our best potential client. He is money in the bank for us, as managers, and we need him if our business is to survive.

The race to find clients is over; now we must take care of those we have. To do that, all parts of the business must work close to the ground. Design, manufacturing — even billing, for nothing is more irritating than to receive an incomprehensible invoice. And as a customer tends to change products at the drop of a hat, the entire business must be organized with him in mind.

It is no longer the scale of the enterprise that counts, but its ability to attract clients, to determine what will please them. And so economies of scale are defunct, producing a lot for no matter whom. They must be replaced with economies of scope: manufacturing products or offering services for specific clients, in a particular field, and modifying them according to the perception we have of those clients.

The client we know best is the one who values us now; it is his tastes and needs that are most accessible to us. And so here is our order of the day: we must expand within our own market. Let us try to produce something that will complement what we produce already.

TO STAY FLEXIBLE, STAY LEAN

Abandoning economies of scale, we must create small units, specializing in two or three products each, so that every employee will know what he is making and will be familiar with the product and the clientele. In that way he will become a kind of expert on the product and will communicate easily with everyone involved in its design, manufacture, presentation, and marketing.

Since technology has become exportable, the grouping

together of businesses is no longer necessary, and large production units are no longer justified. Small, specialized units will facilitate creativity, flexibility, and change.

A good example is that of mini-smelters. No longer working from ore, but from recycled metal, they are not dependent on the existence of raw material in their region. Their electric ovens do not have to be located near coal mines or oil as was the case in past decades. Completely decentralized, they have been set up in the centre of the area they serve, and can adapt rapidly to changes in demand. Because they have not kept up with this new approach, the Americans, once champions of the steel industry, have become, in less than a decade, the least productive in the field: they have clung to outmoded practices and giant installations. They did not foresee the end of economies of scale. On the other hand, Europeans and the Japanese understood that being lean would from now on be one of the hallmarks of good management.

KEEPING YOUR CUSTOMER

In a world where there is no more growth, finding new markets is an almost utopian prospect. In fact, new customers virtually do not exist; the best one can hope for is to steal one away from a competitor. But this strategy is risky, as it is impossible to determine what will lead someone to change one product for another, or to predict what new features our competitor will be introducing tomorrow.

The best way of proceeding is, without doubt, to try to retain our current customers. They are the ones we know best. We are well qualified to trace the evolution of their tastes and needs. They are also our best ambassadors vis-à-vis the consumers who now prefer our competitors' products.

In this context, the size of the business is of no intrinsic interest. What counts is that the size correspond to the market the business can truly serve, the market in which it can truly innovate. A successful business is no longer a commercial giant but one that can serve its market with as few resources as possible. Leanness, sub-contracting, strategic alliances have become the principles managers must honour to remain competitive.

8

THE GALAXY ENTERPRISE

To adapt to their surroundings, businesses
forge alliances that are forever changing.
It is thanks to this state of flux, which is
dynamic, almost chaotic, that they can
adjust to an environment that is in
constant, unpredictable evolution.

Not all businesses remained passive as their economic, political, and social environment mutated. A good example of successful adaptation is Bombardier. Manufacturing skidoos in a difficult market 20 years ago, this company transformed itself into one of the world's great builders of human transport systems. It designed and built passenger and business planes, subways, and pleasure vehicles; participated in the construction of the high-speed train in France and the Airbus; and produced shuttles for the Channel tunnel.

When you visit Bombardier's head office in Montréal, you are struck by the limited size of its personnel. In fact, the role of head office is to harmonize the decisions and tactical moves made by the 50 factories and production centres scattered across North America and Europe.

The head office receives messages from below — the various strategies proposed — then weighs possibilities and shares the resources. Each year those few executives attached to the centre cross the Atlantic dozens of times to visit the production units and to meet not only the managers but also the workers on the assembly lines.

Where Bombardier begins and ends is often difficult to determine. Sometimes it allies itself with companies which in other markets are its fierce competitors. While Bombardier is selling GEC-Alsthom's high-speed train in North America, it's in competition with this same company on the European railway market. The sharing of information has become crucial to management: one must know what information to give out, what to share, and what to keep to oneself. But what is certain is that one can no longer hoard it jealously as though it were a treasure buried in head office.

Other giants, like Johnson & Johnson, seek information and creativity wherever there are people familiar with markets and production. They find a small company with a promising product, buy it, but leave the owner in place who was responsible for its success. There, too, the initiative comes from below, where there are people who know the product, its market, and the technical possibilities. Their knowledge enables them to react promptly, and to be creative.

THE NEW INDUSTRIAL FABRIC

Through his capacity to adapt and his knowledge of the product or byproduct he has to offer, the supplier has become an essential partner in the development of the larger enterprise. Suppliers are sometimes former divisions that the mother company dropped because it could not give them the attention they required to adapt successfully to an ever-changing environment. Once independent, these new small specialized businesses know their world exceedingly well and can adapt speedily. They can act as privileged partners who can help the main company respond effectively to the market.

Large enterprises now jettison those operations where they have no basic expertise and where their relative lack of competence is reflected in lower profits, or even a loss. A giant like Alcan, for instance, sold off Alcan Building Products USA as well as Alcan Building Products Canada, even though they brought in sales in excess of $400 million.

This retrenchment explains the massive layoffs in executive suites over the last two or three years. ABB, the Swiss-Swedish giant, cut its head office personnel by 95%. In Canada, Domtar took measures that were almost as extreme, over a period of three years. The executives were not let go because they were incompetent, but because they had become superfluous. It was no longer necessary to plan, to channel information and instructions from top to bottom in the company. Most decisions were now made elsewhere, within the production units.

Could those executives who had been released hope to find employment in other large companies? Not really. Most would have to resign themselves to starting their own businesses, providing services or manufacturing products, creating networks of small firms that would share information, like Bombardier with its partners — sometimes competing, sometimes collaborating.

Europe experienced this phenomenon when the European Community decided to restructure its steel industry. Thousands of executives were let go throughout the main industrial heartlands of the old continent. What seemed a social catastrophe at the time has turned out to be a very good thing, for these people, competent for the most part, have launched their own businesses, have begun manufacturing products, have initiated procedures that otherwise would have languished in the drawers of large corporations. Their clients? Often their former employers. Their inventions? Everything from a new process for road signs, to paint for extension springs, to preventive maintenance for industrial valves.

The new environment has forced businesses to find good solutions to their problems: by creating difficulties for poorly adapted organizations, it has required them to eliminate everything that was unproductive. These elements — individuals or entire divisions — once liberated from hierarchy and an overweening administration, then could, and had to, be creative and come up with new products and services that would fulfil the needs of the market.

THE NEW SLAVES

And so a new industrial fabric has been put in place, made up of lean and flexible businesses that constantly alter their relationships according to their needs. Stripped-down head offices coordinate the activities of production units, which are managed, more often than not, by specialists either actually involved in or closely allied to production. The local centres often do their own marketing and choose their own style of organization in harmony with policies defined by head office, always leaving room for creativity.

Anything that is not directly linked to the company's primary vocation is sub-contracted to suppliers. They are no longer chosen on the basis of cost, but in terms of the contribution they can make to cultivating the customer. In adopting the objectives of the larger entity, they give proof of their quality and their level of interest. This is how long-term ties are forged between suppliers and clients. Commercial relationships increasingly become bonds of mutual assistance; the small supplier receives advice, technical help, and training from his much larger client.

This world is not necessarily idyllic. Such mutual assistance has not been imposed by right-thinking humanists. Its purpose, rather, is to enhance the profitability of whoever is giving the orders, enabling him to respond more easily and more rapidly to the needs of his own customer. While the supplier is no longer judged according to cost, his imagination is being assessed, as well as his ability to enhance the effectiveness of his client.

The Japanese are familiar with the Toyota slaves, those small auto parts suppliers that must excel in organization, imagination, flexibility, and cost-cutting in order to satisfy the needs of their all-powerful client, which actually puts together the cars. To be granted the privilege of supplying the large company, they must agree, for the most part, to be at its beck and call. That means producing the exact quantities required, when and where they are needed, with very little advance notice. The supplier must deliver the cases of parts to the assembly plants, to the assembly line where they will be used, open and sorted in order to facilitate the work of the assemblers.

What happens if a corporation's customer puts in an order that requires work to start Monday morning? The order is accepted because the large company knows it can count on its supplier to provide it with the parts it needs. Which means that, on the basis of a single telephone call Saturday morning, a small business must recall its employees over the weekend to produce the necessary parts before Monday morning. That is part of the deal.

In Europe, as in the United States and Canada, suppliers that specialize in last-minute quality production are legion.

In fact, big business has passed on to them its problems with quality, storage, and organization of labour that it no longer wants to handle. It no longer wants to deal with them because it had become too inflexible to cater to the needs of today's customers and to compete globally.

ACTION ABOVE ALL

Managers presently are poorly prepared for this new environment. Traditional schooling persists in teaching managers how to reflect, plan, and organize, rather than how to act. Faced with a problem, the manager is supposed to back off and think. In a centralized business, he sends the problem upstairs, and, as it usually involves a number of disciplines, a committee must be formed so that experts in supply, marketing, computer science, insurance, and who knows what else, can have their say. Today, in a universe where everything is in flux, one must be able to jump on the train while it is still in motion. We must always be willing to change the way we do things, to alter our forecasts. It is no longer thinkers we need, but people who act and solve problems. We do not indoctrinate employees, we give them information and the means to act so they can find and implement solutions on their own.

Does that mean a manager must no longer think? No. On the contrary, he must have enough experience in his field to know in advance the ways in which he can act and react. For him, to reflect is no longer to meditate upon action. He never stops reflecting. He is like the captain in the storm, who must think *as* he acts, because he cannot foresee most of what will change in his environment.

All this, of course, has important implications when it comes to designing a business. The decision-makers — all employees have become decision-makers — must not, as before, wait for orders from head office. At most, the directors must provide employees with an overall view of how the business should evolve and a context within which this is to take place. But within this context, the employees must make their own decisions and take their own actions. The importance given to action spells the end of hierarchy: the army of executives there to pass on orders and then verify if they've been carried out is henceforth superfluous. The tasks of planning, direction, and control are much less important now than the need for quick decisions and rapid action.

The purpose of this speed, this sense of urgency, is to respond swiftly to the client's needs and avoid a request's moving uselessly up the ladder in the hierarchy. As soon as it reaches someone who can fulfil the need, he must take the necessary decisions, while honouring the ground rules laid down by the head office. It is crucial, of course, that the directors be certain of the technical competence and innovative spirit of its employees and of middle management. In practice, the latter will refer only difficult cases to the top: their aim is to resolve as many problems, and emergencies, as possible, so that the directors can concentrate on questions that truly concern the entire company.

In the past, change was regarded as a threat. Now, change is part and parcel of management. A manager is no longer judged on the kind of decision he takes, but on the way in which he sees decisions carried out.

That is the second fundamental difference that modern competition has made. Creativity has supplanted planning, and now action takes centre stage, to the near exclusion of reflection. The state of chaos that defines our present world requires that creativity and action go hand in hand.

In the meantime, business is being subjected to a dismemberment. The hierarchy is shrinking, and tasks are devolving to operating units. Decentralization is the order of the day. There is no point in being creative if one cannot act. It's impossible to act if one is not creative. Thought and action increasingly overlap, and that is where responsibility comes into play.

In the modern enterprise, we leaders must avoid the trap of overseeing decisions. Rather, we must take their measure and appreciate their being carried out.

9

CHAOS RESPONDS TO CHAOS

*Proximity to markets, limited size, modest goals,
creativity and flexibility, sustained effort: these are the
virtues that make for success in business today.*

Management is far from being an exact science: its principles are not dogma. On the contrary, management is the art of adapting one's business to its economic, political, and social environment. To succeed in this, the manager must rely on his view of that environment. Such a view is not the fruit of exhaustive analysis but simply a general understanding that seems to explain most of the current developments in the life of the enterprise. If this understanding is a good match with reality, the manager and his business will live in harmony with the economic, political, and social environment. If not, crises will abound and solutions will no longer work; both managers and employees will find themselves in disarray. That is what happens when the surroundings change significantly and the manager takes no notice. That is what is happening today.

But one must recognize that the symbiosis between one's views of the world and one's own actions is a powerful source of progress. Just as a past generation saw the consolidation of an extraordinary equilibrium between the evolution of the social and economic environment and managers' views and consequently their behaviour, so a new order will certainly appear. But nostalgic though we may be, the old views no longer apply. How should we deal with all this?

First let us remember how deep rooted this old order was. At the risk of repeating myself, our civilization over the last 40 years or so was marked by unusual growth prospects and stability. Politicians, intellectuals, managers, entrepreneurs, public servants, all collaborated in creating structures that avoided the changes, upheavals, and crises so feared by entrepreneurs and consumers alike. Order evolved as managers, policy makers, and the underlying prospects of the economy worked in tandem. Order here meant a virtuous circle. The environment produced incentives which, when responded to effectively, further reinforced both the incentives and the model used to react to them.

It may not be surprising that the United States became the hotbed of so-called modern management techniques. The use of one language and a single currency in a market of 200 million people living under the same government made it possible for both stability and growth to flourish. Management methods based on planning, organization, and control emerged and were refined to a high degree.

Since these techniques worked well, Harvard University took them as a model for its own teaching method, which made generous use of case studies, for it assumed that a technique that had provided good results in one situation would be equally successful under similar circumstances. That proved true as long as the economy was expanding. New markets were available; procedures and decisions therefore did not have to be very refined to give adequate returns. The aim was to produce in great quantity rather than to manufacture good products meticulously designed for the customer. The demand was so great that consumers would have bought almost anything.

THOUGHT AND INDOCTRINATION

Since this view of the environment and of management required the channelling of all the company's resources into the rapid production of standardized products, the role of employees was to carry out what directors decided to do. All the company's actions grew out of a cast of mind dedicated to planning. The executives, who functioned as preachers, were responsible for mobilizing everyone's energies in order to attain the chosen goal. Management, in a nutshell, consisted of thought, mobilization, and execution. If problems arose, external consultants were hired to help the owner think things out, and plan. Solutions were born in the head; their application was taken for granted. Thought and action were two quite distinct functions, the first dominating the second. This logic was carried to an extreme with the creation of think tanks, entities totally divorced from action. Their proliferation was founded, essentially, in the growing vogue for reflection and the reverence for thought.

Since the key to a well-run business was to recruit all the personnel for the same project, we worked out a number of ways to ensure that everyone would conform. For the most part these consisted of gentle measures such as salary increases, attractive retirement plans, a shorter work week, and so on. For the employee, the goal was not to improve production, but to remain in the company.

Schools of management hired professors of psychology and sociology to study the best way of exerting power and control in an organization. For the organization now overshadowed the business. Everything was organized and planned so all energies could be consolidated and the enterprise could grow more rapidly than that of the competitor. The principles taught at Harvard and other management schools were elevated to the rank of scientific truths.

To be fair, while the business schools' main curriculum still proceeds from the notion of order, there are some signs here and there of a new management approach, and they are growing in number. Henry Mintzberg at McGill University has been dealing with the futility of planning (as a substitute for strategy) for a long time. Brenda Zimmerman of York University has gone out of her way to contrast the so-called equilibrious view of the world to that of an ever-changing process. She has written: "In chaos theory . . . a healthy organization never approaches an equilibrious state. It is unpredictable, ever-changing, and complex. At any given moment there really is order, but the order is self-organized rather than imposed from above."

But everything comes to an end, every system carries within it the seeds of its own destruction. We understood too late that in seeking stability and uniformity in our economic, political, and social structures, we brought about the globalization of markets: the slightest incident at one end of the planet now had repercussions all over the world that were rapid and impossible to foresee. Neither distances nor borders nor tariffs could protect anyone, any longer, from his competitors, wherever they might be. The end of economic growth only exacerbated this competition, for which we were not prepared.

In an effort to do away with uncertainty, we re-created chaos, and suddenly we became aware that our vision of a plannable world no longer corresponded with reality.

Our mistake became brutally obvious once markets ceased to expand, and we saw great corporations, not racing side by side in pursuit of new markets but standing face to face deep in a dead end. The Mastodons designed for running in a straight line now had to compete on a tortuous obstacle course. And soon small competitors appeared, ultralight, quick to change direction and adapt to shifts in the terrain, to infiltrate nooks and crannies of the market where the giants could not squeeze in. It began to resemble the rout of the powerful American army by the elusive Vietcong.

PREACH NO MORE, ACT!

Since the survival of a business depends on its ability to adapt to the unpredictable, the entrepreneur is once more gaining ground on the manager. A direct descendant of the craftsman, he knows his customer and his product and can quickly match the second with the first. Intimate with those responsible for design and production, he makes sure they remain in close touch, so as to facilitate rapid change. He knows how to make sales staff, engineers, and those charged with production work closely together, and he knows change can come from anywhere: a new concept, a new process, a new material, a new sales method.

The job of a manager is no longer to preach, but to solve problems as they present themselves.

There is no longer any question of separating the company's operations into airtight compartments. On the contrary, they must come together into teams committed to specific projects that will be dissolved and reconstituted differently as soon as their purpose becomes superfluous. The new management must be concerned with action rather than planning, must opt for change, and not hold tight to continuity. If change was once a threat to the company's effectiveness, it must now be seen as something one has to accept in adapting to chaos. As Mintzberg says, "Strategy emerges from action."

The new entrepreneur will have to eliminate anything that separates him from his production teams, his goal being not to control them but to stimulate them, to accelerate change. During a storm, the captain maintains direct contact with the engine room, bypassing the entire hierarchy of the ship. The hierarchical pyramid is going to disappear. No more hierarchy, no more division of labour, no more planning and control, all sacred principles taught in schools of management. We have passed from the era of power to that of knowledge.

That last sentence merits closer examination. In the old environment, power was the mainspring of action. It shaped the business, the organization. Today, power has perhaps become superfluous; in any case, it is subservient to knowledge. A nimble enterprise, decentralized and close to its clientele, relies on the capacity of its work teams to act quickly and well. Such competence is not invoked through orders: only knowledge makes it possible. Experience begets intuition, which makes it possible to act immediately, without long reflection or prior planning. That is why knowledge is important.

Governments may say what they want, but they too are affected by the globalization of markets and must become creative and efficient if they want to keep business within their borders. Countries or regions will pay dearly if they rely on simple financial incentives, for businesses more and more seek conditions that facilitate flexibility and creativity. The calibre of human resources is an important consideration in choosing a site. Managers look for those who can act, react, and respond in an original way to novel situations.

THREE CONCLUSIONS

1) Decentralize to respond instantly to the marketplace
Businesses will be torn between the need to specialize in
order to satisfy a very difficult clientele, and the temptation
to expand their product line so as to take advantage of wide-
ranging economies.

Those who choose specialization doubtless will experience difficulties in reconciling change and continuity.
Preceding chapters have shown how ephemeral and impul-
sive the tastes of consumers have become. The specialized
business must therefore follow very closely, and if possible
anticipate, the needs of a volatile market. For specialists can
no longer be satisfied with manufacturing items of very high
quality, or even with responding to their clients' expectations; they must innovate on their own and offer consumers
products they would never have thought of but tomorrow
will demand. The challenge in managing such businesses
will be to stay the course, and despite constant modifications
to their products, to keep to the same niche in the market,
without diversifying. To innovate within self-imposed
limits: that is the challenge for specialized businesses.

On the other hand, those large corporations that *have*
chosen to diversify must resolve another problem: that of
performing well while constantly manufacturing different
products. As discussed above, they must replace economies
of scale with economies of scope. In other words, they must
extend the range of products they can offer different
segments of their market, profiting from the fact that they
know their clients well to furnish them with more items
adapted to their needs. They will run the inevitable risk of
launching products that won't succeed, and must be able to
let them drop, in order to try again.

These businesses will have to both foster creativity and

ensure the coordination of their operations. The problem in managing diversified companies will derive from the need to do things well while constantly creating and abandoning new products. To do things well is relatively easy in a company whose products change very little. It becomes a real challenge when one is continually bringing forth new products and letting others fall by the wayside. What is more, creativity is difficult to reconcile with the rigid strictures imposed by quality manufacturing. The challenge for managers in diversified industries will be to accommodate mass production to a constant turnover of products.

Whether the business is specialized or diversified, the solution to its problems will in either case be decentralization. Creative teams, manufacturing teams, marketing teams, sales teams, will all react swiftly to signals sent out by the market, while the head office will be responsible for harmony and cohesion: it will share out resources; foster the company's image and its links with the community, governments, and investors; and will establish the ground rules for acquisitions and alliances.

2) Take a slimming cure

Head-office activities do not require a large staff. Just a handful of specialists in financing, taxes, accounting, as well as a few people with in-depth knowledge of all those sectors in which the company plays a role. At least one person at head office must be totally familiar with each division. We can see to what extent the size of head office can be controlled.

Production units must also take a slimming cure. Market volatility will no longer allow us to rely on economies of scale: production could never reach sufficient volume before products would have to be replaced.

Let us then give up on our old dream of mass production,

for the more we grow, the more we grow away from the needs of the customer, and the more we become bureaucratized. Bureaucracy encourages collective procrastination, division of labour, hierarchy.

Let us renounce economies of scale, for in a large company, an operation that results in 5% of the profits will receive less attention than one that produces 30%. We must therefore jettison the first so we can concentrate on the second. All power to small, flexible production units that can answer to the needs of micro-markets. The challenge to big business is to follow that example.

3) Foster creativity at all levels

We must make the transition from the dominance of power to the dominance of knowledge. The commandments and incantations of upper management must give way to the inspiration of people in the field, because they are the ones who know market conditions best, and how to respond to them.

In any case, people who work in companies have different cultures, different values, and different aspirations. You can no longer indoctrinate them; they will not allow it. People now see business as a means to realizing their personal aspirations. And that will be more and more the case, since the flexibility markets demand will remove the barrier between private and professional life. No more nine to five. There will no longer be a time for work and a time for leisure. And personal fulfilment — never a priority for a boss giving orders — can only be offered by someone who motivates and helps bring results, who fosters creativity.

We have come full circle: planning is rendered pointless by the fickle chaos surrounding us, which in its turn elicits personal initiative and creativity, resulting in actions that are unpredictable but beneficial for the company.

Thus chaos responds to chaos.

10

THE LAMPLIGHTER

The post-war years, with their vision of unending progress,
fostered the emergence of a number of key concepts, soon
elevated to the status of precepts for action in total symbiosis
one with another. Not only business leaders, but governments
and their policies as well, were part of the perfect picture.
Today those same governments are in disarray.

If some businesses were slow, in the past, to master the basics of organization, the transition was still very rapid, and under the aegis of major national and international institutions whose role was to assure the economy's stability, the transformation soon took hold. Today business is reeling under the onslaught of chaos. If it wants to survive, it has no choice but to adapt and to take all possible measures that will enable it to do so.

To read the business pages, whether local, national, or international, is to come across numerous experiments, sometimes painful ones, undertaken by a host of businesses seeking to improve their situation. Decentralization, a crucial factor in creativity, has now become a universal imperative, as decreed by prophets such as Peter Drucker, proclaimed by gurus such as Tom Peters, and applied by a large number of businesses or anonymous practitioners.

While in the past enlightened minds prevailed on

governments to form the UN, GATT, and the IMF to create order in a world that needed it, today the powers-that-be lag far behind in their response to chaos and unrest. If there is to be a new symbiosis, a new understanding, governments cannot afford to miss the boat. If they have been slow, so far, to grasp what is at stake, the constraints that lie before them will force them to adapt, although by then the costs will likely be even higher.

PUBLIC ORDER IN DISARRAY

Business is familiar with chaos. A favourite refrain in Chambers of Commerce now is "The future is not what it was." Business reacts because it is given its cue by the markets.

On the other hand, the world of politics and government, still coasting on past success — real or imagined — persists in adhering to precepts that no longer apply. With the pressure on public monies in the West, planning is giving way to improvisation, but always with the same insistence on preserving the system as it is. Worse still, the belt-tightening brings with it even greater control.

However, there, too, chaos is having its effect. In truth, the subjects no longer obey the king. The laws, the excessive taxes, the finicky regulations have spawned a veritable industry of evasion that strips legislation of all its legitimacy. Black markets are flourishing; tax evasion is a destabilizing force. What the government wants, it no longer has the means to demand. Its boat is drifting into the reefs, and it is short on fuel.

There again, things will have to change. The bases for action, the goals pursued, have been rejected by the populace, if not thwarted altogether. In a free society, you don't put people on a leash. New objectives that make for a consensus will have to be devised.

THE ALLEGORY OF THE LAMPLIGHTER

The unemployment rate remains a serious concern. The industrial transition through which we are passing is not without its hardships. Countries that were long admired and praised for their policies of full employment are now prey to unemployment of unanticipated proportions. The noose has tightened around them cruelly; there seems no way out. The scope of the problem cries out for correctives, but suggested remedies always imply recourse to the same old methods, newly refurbished, a bit like a conditioned reflex. Such an attitude only exacerbates the crisis and worsens its consequences. To delay and resist adapting will only increase the terrible human costs. To invest in the preservation of the existing structure will only further deplete the few resources left to help those who are paying the price for the necessary transition. Have we hoodwinked the men and women drawn to jobs that have turned out to be precarious? Must we try to stimulate the economy artificially, so as to preserve employment?

In times past, cities were lit by gas, a form of energy that was not self-activating. And so lamplighters walked through the streets, lighting the lamps at the desired hour and putting them out at dawn, so as not to waste fuel. Imagine for a moment that electricity had only come on the scene in 1980 or 1990. The laying off of lamplighters would have given rise to numerous protests citing security of employment, and the firings, in violation of acquired rights, would most certainly have been the object of indignant outcries.

What is the difference between the gas lamp and a train, the hand-sorting of mail, or a soldering workshop? Only the passing of time makes the allegory of the lamplighter seem more telling. Today one would rightly claim that to protect the jobs of lamplighters would deplete resources that could

be applied to creating other jobs. Maintaining gas lamps
would have delayed the electrification of the streets! But
overall, we have no clear idea of the number of jobs lost,
because of the jobs we have retained or created artificially.

GLOBALIZATION RESULTS IN GROWING REGIONALIZATION

As Kenichi Ohmae has claimed in *The Borderless World*, in
a world without borders the nation-state has lost most of its
added value. Its role and its purpose have been greatly diminished if not eliminated altogether. Local governments, on the
other hand, because they are so close to their constituency,
must respond to the pressures and demands of the populace.

Our modern societies are curiously paradoxical: globalization is there, although no one wanted it, an implacable,
irresistible reality. But at the same time, regionalisms are
growing and multiplying. John Naisbitt, the guru of current
trends, has documented this phenomenon well. The most
casual eye can see it all around: cultural, ethnic, and linguis-
tic differences are being asserted where we hardly knew they
existed. We are in the planetary age: planetary vision, local
application.

Now central governments are committing the same sin of
excess as business during the 1980s. They have lost their
sense of purpose and are back at square one: they are
burdened with a multi-level hierarchy and alienated from
their true client, who must deal with his monarch via
persons and groups blocking the way. The principal occupa-
tion of bureaucrats seems to consist in pondering and reflecting so as to devise action plans, policies, and directives that
will provide standardized, uniform services to all with no
respect for local differences.

But the answer is on its way. As was the case with

business, government will have to adapt because it is beginning to come apart at the seams. It can no longer rally the support of the majority of the population; its determination to maintain order — once greatly enhanced by its power of taxation — is creating growing disorder. The government is up against chaos, and its old powers of persuasion can no longer help it out of a difficult situation. On the contrary, they are now counterproductive.

The coming solution will be found in the political decentralization that is emerging everywhere. To confer on local governments certain of its national services will force the legislative machine to be sensitive to the opinions of citizens and their awareness of their responsibilities. At the same time, cutbacks will be initiated in a thousand different ways. We should be happy about this: it will give us the opportunity to try things, to experiment, and to vary our approach.

Certainly we might have hoped that our symbiosis with the new environment would have come about more quickly, and that government would have jumped on the bandwagon at the same time as business, but there you have it, that's chaos!

11

NEW GUIDEPOSTS

To navigate a storm is not so bad; sometimes it's essential and rewarding. Certainly the conquest of Everest was a more glorious challenge, more impressive and culturally more prestigious. But every era must define itself in terms of the specific constraints imposed on it. In truth, it is the constraints that provide the challenge, and not the opposite.

If Davy Crockett set out to vanquish an army all on his own, Indiana Jones made it very clear that you only lay eyes on your treasure after having survived many ordeals. To adapt to new conditions, one must first change one's outlook.

The contrast between Davy Crockett and Indiana Jones shows that different challenges make for different heroes. The leader of the old economy had to rally his team for the conquest of Everest; there were no other heroic acts possible. The leader of the new economy mobilizes his forces to clear the obstacles and finish the course before anyone else. From now on, his performance will be measured against those around him, rather than his own ambitions.

Whether we are managers in the private or public sector, entrepreneurs, or professionals, we all have to make choices in order to act. And these strategic choices, these business decisions, have nothing whatever to do in the final analysis with the mastery of advanced methods or expert systems. Certainly these latter deserve serious attention, but we know there is no single solution: the decision-maker must choose among claims by specialists that are often contradictory. What he has to fall back on are his own principles, general and specific, and his own intuition and experience. In the isolation booth of decision-making, variables and criteria are reduced to a strict minimum.

That is what I have tried to point out in this book. I have tried to shed light on the nature of the old economy, on post-war society, and its impact on businesses and organizations. I have then contrasted that society with today's, to conclude that new guideposts are beginning to emerge. Which led me to juxtapose Everest with a storm at sea.

I wanted to influence attitudes and perceptions. And it is with that in mind that I make my appeal. It's easy to gripe about the recent recession that has plagued the world and to dream of a magic wand that will whisk us back to 1960. But we are now entering a period of transition in which the principles of the new economy will prevail even among the most recalcitrant.

We must therefore adapt, hone our instincts, set our sights on new markers. We must master new rules and learn to communicate them. Once again, that is what I've tried to do. I wanted my book, unlike others on the subject, to portray the building as a whole without rummaging around in all the closets. It's the building one sees first; the architect is the first to be consulted.

I am not denying the importance of books that are more descriptive and complete, but I am wary of them. Tom Peters provides a good example. Would he have written about chaos had he not covered himself in shame by proposing models to emulate, in *In Search of Excellence*, models which failed shortly after publication? I contend that we must change our outlook.

SMALL VERITIES

When I became a professor at l'École des Hautes Études Commerciales in Montréal, armed with my degree from the American university which was the most demanding in formalism and mathematics, I was, all the same, taken aback by the basic schooling given to students in business administration. It had become so formalized, there was so much emphasis on method, that content was almost totally absent. I therefore got permission to try a new formula: I wanted my students to understand the simple facts of economic life. I asked them questions. If doctors were paid a salary, what effect would that have on health care? How do we explain that marijuana sells for $100 an ounce when it only costs a few cents to produce? Why are public ventures inefficient? All that seemed, and still seems, to me, much more important than to calculate the marginal rate of substitution between bread and meat, when it's not specified whether the former is whole wheat or the latter is beef or fowl.

I should state that business schools tend to be open to the world in a way that is rare in a university milieu. I was extremely fortunate to have been trained in economics in management schools. L'École des Hautes Études Commerciales in Montréal, the Graduate School of Industrial Administration at Carnegie-Mellon University, and the Graduate School of Management at the University of Rochester all shared a common denominator. Alongside rather formal teaching and curricula existed a basic respect for facts, or behaviour, to be exact, especially at Carnegie-Mellon. These schools did not hold fast to the hermetic rigour so prized in more staid institutions.

It is not unusual for academics — in fact this may be a requirement for their success — to interpret facts in terms of theory. Economics is not immune to this approach.

However, the study of economics in a business-school environment confronts reality from all sides. Together with traditional subjects like finance, economics, and accounting, less conventional disciplines, like sociology and psychology, are integrated into the curriculum. There even exist non-disciplines: organizational theory is more a focus of attention than a corpus of knowledge.

Furthermore, business schools' economists tend to be regarded with suspicion by their colleagues in traditional university departments; they are notorious for their "delinquent" character. The business-school environment can be an excellent curative for complacency, as it favours constant scepticism and inquiry. No one could be blind to the impact of facts on ideas. So much so that some of the truths arrived at by economists, in particular, began even then to break down, or, to be more precise, to take another form.

Most seriously discredited were those precepts that had been handed down from the interventionist period. Rules and regulations, fiscal and monetary management, all were given a rough time. It had been thought that one could chart a course for the economy or society while disregarding certain natural laws that presumably had been overcome.

In fact, a cerebral and reductionist approach had prevailed over flair and intuition. The social sciences, and economics in particular, increasingly favoured interventionism, to the detriment of spontaneity. Intellectuals became increasingly contemptuous of the business community, and of entrepreneurs. They judged them on their own intellectual terms and took notice of no others. Business people and the entrepreneurial class were considered ignorant, or poorly informed. The idea was that interventionism would impose order. This trend permeated business schools, which came up with numerous formulas designed to do away with uncertainty and be a comfort to managers. Technique, so it was thought, could take over from judgement.

Another good example is the Harvard model of business policy, well known to anyone having attended a school of management. In analysing the environment, one discerns opportunities. One's strengths and weaknesses are weighed in the balance, and then one takes the plunge. This model was perfectly suited to the old economy, and its principles were tried and true. But if our reading of today's society and economy is made according to the same guidelines, then we're finished. If we do not take into consideration the basic fact that businesses and organizations are the product of a culture, of decisions made, actions undertaken, and the environment, all interacting, then we will make a serious error: we will convince ourselves that these organizations are eternal, that they have no need to shift their perspective.

The theory of relativity taught us that an observer's position influences his perception of the universe. Traditional schooling in business, and the guidelines of the old economy, encouraged the belief that such relativity did not exist, whereas in fact it is more insidious today than ever. What is more, the way in which one views the universe, changes the universe.

The businesses and institutions that we built in perfect harmony with the environment, or so we thought, helped .ter that environment. The idea is well known. George Sorros, the L.llionaire broker and speculator, stated in an interview he gave to *The Economist* that he made his fortune by applying a very simple principle: that our understanding of the universe influences the universe, which in turn influences our understanding. And so if you can decode the understanding of others, you have a good chance of knowing how things will evolve.

We must therefore see businesses, along with public, private, and union organizations, as forms adapting to a social, economic, and political environment, while at the same time adapting that environment to themselves. We must transcend the model of business policy, and look at how organizations, responding to changes in the environment, will modify it in turn and alter the signals it is sending back to the world of business.

It is this reciprocal relationship of retroactive influences that led me, during my last years as an academic, to question the Harvard model, and above all the precepts of the old economy. Because they derived from a specific symbiosis between business and the economy, these precepts were, by definition, temporary. Already, at the end of the 1960s, the edifice was beginning to crumble.

While I have always been fascinated by formalism, I reserved judgement on many issues because human interaction always provides surprises. At the risk of oversimplifying, the world may be said to be divided between those who know what *should* happen and those who aspire to know what *will* happen.

The former tend to extrapolate from their formalism and derive prescriptions from theoretical models. They are normative, and imbued with a view of the world as they think it should be; they impose their solutions. In particular, they try to manipulate people and their behaviour so that theory will become reality. And what follows are perverse effects and unanticipated consequences. What has been proposed or prescribed does not occur, because the system of incentive has altered, and people have moved off in another direction.

The latter are less inclined to change the world than to capitalize on their understanding of it. Machiavelli is certainly a good example. Such people are well suited to business, because business requires a vision of what is likely to happen, in order to define what might be possible for a given company. Out of this comes a strategy, and objectives to pursue.

There are immutable laws like gravity or the law of supply and demand. They apply everywhere. A society's welfare or a company's success will follow from these laws, depending on how people organize themselves and what the set of incentives is.

I was fortunate to be an agnostic of sorts. I became intrigued by unanticipated consequences. The law of demand and supply was as valid in Russia as in the United States, but there was a winning combination in the latter country. This dialectic in economics played out within a business school gave me an unprecedented opportunity to widen my understanding of the old economy and its limitations. A colleague and I designed a course called "Economy and Organization." Today such a title is easy to grasp, but our initial approach was intuitive. We set out to compare and contrast a number of models from different periods or societies, so as to better understand the dynamics of our own period and bring to the fore certain significant contradictions that have since become clear to all.

The encounter between my own questionings and apprehensions, and the real world — where action and decision-making are closely entwined — enhanced my understanding of the new economy once I was out in the workforce myself. I joined the National Bank of Canada in 1984. In many respects the banking industry was a sterling example of the old economy and its organization. This was to be expected. Banks fed themselves on growth; we looked on them more in terms of their asset growth than their profitability. The conventional measure was returns on assets, as if this was a proxy for returns on shareholder capital. But more importantly, does not a bank define itself in terms of its stability? It is duty-bound to be the most stable object in the industrial landscape, in an environment that sets great store by stability.

What is more, the way in which the Canadian banking system evolved, well circumscribed by government policy and regulation, put great emphasis on efficient performance. It was and probably still is one of the most effective banking systems in the world, considering the difficulties posed by the enormous Canadian land mass. It put great emphasis on delivering a rather wide range of services through a multiple branch system that required massive coordination. As computer systems were still in their infancy, banks provided clients with a thorough and almost error-free service. This was in great part the result of a longstanding management policy of uniformity. Permanent directives on procedures were distributed to employees, who followed them religiously. Management was top heavy, as was to be expected, given the scale of the operation.

In a simpler world, with limited competition, this system produced good results. But then, gradually, the banking system opened up, expanding its services and products. The competition from non-banking companies transformed the sector. Complexity ensued and so did the attempts to deal with it. Certainly the new economy, even before we had a name for it, brought about these transformations. Added value in banking is a matter of personal judgement of clients and the ability to process a huge number of transactions swiftly. Therefore as the knowledge-based economy expanded, banks adjusted, with knowledge as their raw material. Peter Drucker argues that knowledge is the most distinctive feature of the world in which we live.

So while it is customary from the outside to view banks as solid and stable, the industry has undergone a major facelift. It is not appropriate for me to talk of the competition, so I will restrict myself to the National Bank of Canada. Others have seen the change it has undergone and have viewed it differently and for different reasons. But for me personally, the sound scepticism fostered during my academic life stood me in good stead. My preoccupation with organizations and their necessity to live in symbiosis with their environment met the challenge of a changing world. And there has been no lack of turbulence in the banking industry in the last fifteen years.

My transition from the academic world to the world of banking was not without its ups and downs. The experienced professor, learning his craft, had to develop new reflexes.

I believe I have contributed to the transformation of the National Bank and have helped it adapt to changes in the banking sector, but I was lucky, because it so happened that the National Bank was well disposed to taking new directions. Not only was it known, by its clients, to be creative and flexible, it also boasted a tradition of change that was an integral part of its identity. It both welcomed changes and was selective in its choice of them.

Today there is nothing novel in talking about one's client rather than one's projects. Magazines and journals are filled with articles on communicating with the client. It has also become fashionable to talk of decentralization, and of taking slimming cures. The National Bank made these choices long before they became popular. And so, it happens, have many of its clients.